WHO THE HELL IS IMRE LODBROG?

Sébastien Régnier
Barbara Browning

Outpost19 | San Francisco
outpost19.com

Browning, Barbara and Régnier, Sébastien
        Who The Hell Is Imre Lodbrog? / Barbara
Browning and Sébastien Régnier
        ISBN: 9781944853389 (pbk)

cover photo: Gregory Hervelin

OUTPOST19

ORIGINAL
PROVOCATIVE
READING

WHO THE HELL IS IMRE LODBROG?

Dedications

Dear Freddy,

I got that postcard you sent of Liz Taylor and Richard Burton passing through Cherbourg. I was happy to get a sign from you – I wasn't expecting one. If I had a return address, I would have answered the old-fashioned way, by post. But since our last Cherbourgian adventures, all my efforts to contact you were in vain. The line was cut. So, here you go: in answer to the question "Who the Hell is Imre Lodbrog?" I chose to tell my life passing through yours, the story of our understated friendship, across forty years of undercover rock 'n' roll. If this book ever falls into your hands, I hope you'll see in it the homage I wanted to pay to the man and the artist you are. Both stainless. But talent and glory don't always go hand in hand, as we know very well. I owed you this. Without you, Imre Lodbrog would never have seen the light of day...

Here's to you, Freddy, wild and tender man, immense guitarist. May the evening of your life bring along his lamp, as Joubert used to say.

– Seb

Dear Imre,

For my part, this is for you.

– Barbara

Chapter 1
Who the Hell is Imre Lodbrog?

WHO THE HELL IS IMRE LODBROG?

Maybe I should tell you what I once told Imre in an email before we met. I said, "I was thinking about the appeal of your music and I think it's that you sound like an actor playing the role of an aging rock star, which is precisely the appeal of Leonard Cohen and Bob Dylan, not to mention Serge Gainsbourg and Léo Ferré." I also could have mentioned Iggy Pop. Imre once told me that he'd played my ukulele cover of one of his own songs for a well-known musical friend of his whose opinion he valued, and this person had expressed enthusiasm. I felt quite certain that he was talking about Iggy Pop. It seemed so likely that they'd be friends.

Should I tell you how I came to know Imre? He actually stalked me first. I have a little habit of posting these ukulele cover tunes online. Habit is perhaps an understatement. I've posted something like four hundred of them. I don't do it to seek recognition as a musician – quite frankly, my skills are minimal – like my arrangements. I generally make these covers as small gifts for people, and I float them there in the ether of the Internet. Sometimes I post one without any particular intended recipient, just as a sort of message in a bottle. There are quite a few bobbing around out there like that. One day I noticed that some character had begun leaving short, enigmatic comments on my tracks. There was one, a banal little pop song that made reference to trying to "keep Paris on my mind," and Imre had quietly left a note there saying that I was on Paris's mind, *"je vous assure."* I thought that was sweet. I clicked on his tiny icon and it blew up to reveal a somewhat craggy, wizened face, strategically obscured by a pair of rock star shades:

Interesting.

I played one of his tracks, and then another. Oops. I'd fallen down the rabbit hole. Like me, he seemed to be a little terrifyingly productive. But in his case, the proliferating tracks were all originals (ranging in style from ska to psychobilly) , and in fact it was precisely their originality that was so dizzying. Most of the lyrics were in French, some in a quirky Franglais – all teeming with clever wordplay that didn't diminish their bleak emotional force – or occasional political bite. His voice was low and scratchy, and sometimes he'd double it with a weird, tremulous falsetto that gave you the impression of a blurry photo. It was very appealing. He played rhythm guitar, and evidently slide as well (no other musicians were credited). The drums sounded canned, but he'd programmed in some comical breaks that made you imagine a big hairy gorilla wielding the sticks. In sum – both his sound and his words were an inscrutable mix of humor, incisive intelligence – and something very sad.

I'd obviously struck a goldmine.

And then there was that name. Somebody had to have made that up. The most obvious conclusion to draw was that he was a character invented by my friend, the novelist Harry Mathews. And in fact Harry had told me he was working on a new novel, so that seemed all the more plausible – but when I asked him outright if he was responsible for Lodbrog, he denied it. Of course he could be lying – that's happened before – but he seemed so genuinely mystified by my question. Also, he hardly could have concocted that enormous treasure trove of songs… The second most likely scenario was that I'd imagined Imre Lodbrog myself, but in fact I knew that not to be the case. Still, the name definitely looked like something I could have made up, or, to be honest, something I could have pilfered from an online anagram generator I use with some regularity. Just to see what it might have been derived from, I ran it back through said generator, and retrieved:

BRIDLE GROOM
BOREDOM GIRL

all of which seemed weirdly appropriate.

Then, of course, I did the obvious thing: I Googled him. It just led me back to where I'd come from: his own musical tracks, posted up on the same vaporous cloud where he'd found me – and a few YouTube videos as well, where he certainly looked like an aging rock star. Why wasn't he more famous? The guy was clearly a genius. Harry agreed that he was "terrific." One of the YouTube videos purported to be a "studio session" of the "Lodbrog Bros." filmed in Barcelona. They were playing what appeared to be their hit single, "60 Piges." Four handsome, craggy guys nonchalantly stumbling through a tune about turning sixty – which seemed to be roughly their own vintage. I sent the link of this video to my best friend, saying, "This is my new stalker." She said, "Cute. Where do we meet them? I want the one in the chair with the towel on his head." I said, "Imre seems to live in Paris, but I hate to break it to you, I don't think those are his brothers. I think they're all Imre." It took me a minute to figure this out myself, but the resemblance was just too uncanny. It seems he knew how to use a green screen.

When I reported this conversation to Imre, I said, "If I'm wrong, tell your brother not to get too excited. My best friend is married to a handsome movie star, and besides, she's not really a risk-taker. I think she was joking." He gave no indication of disappointment. He also neither denied nor confirmed the fictional status of the "Lodbrog Bros."

There are lots of things I mention or ask in my emails to which Imre doesn't respond. At first, when I asked him who the hell he was, he responded that it was a long story, perhaps best told by a fire with a good bottle of Vouvray. He did confess to having made up his own name, and told me that Lodbrog was a famous Viking. I'd already figured that out from my Google search, but Imre added an interesting fact that wasn't on the Lodbrog Wikipedia page: his namesake had died in a pit of vipers.

Perhaps you find it an exaggeration to call Imre my stalker. After all, a lot of people leave comments on the things we all post online. The technical term for someone who asks to be alerted to your posts is a "follower". Imre was following me, and once I figured out how interesting his music was, I began following him as well. I don't follow everyone who follows me. But if somebody starts stalking me, I tend to stalk them back with a vengeance.

The turning point was when I logged on one day and saw he'd posted a new track with the brief and curious title, "Browning." Needless to say, I clicked on it. Most people associate my name with the poet – or one of the poets, either Elizabeth Barrett or Robert. I'm not sure anybody else has ever associated my last name with the gun manufacturer, but Imre had. He called me a "killer." I liked it. Another French guy left a little comment calling Imre an "old fox," and asking, "did she listen to your song?" Imre just said, "Who?"

That was cute.

I decided to avenge myself. I whipped off a cover of one of Imre's songs, one with evidently anti-capitalist content. I tried to reproduce a bit of the dark cynicism of the original. I posted it without commentary. Imre left a note indicating that he was disoriented. I told him when one felt lost it was always a good idea to go left. Of course I meant this in the political sense. I was pretty sure we were on the same side. It wasn't long before we were working in collusion.

He suggested a duet on the classic theme of Beauty and the Beast. Imre is something of a classicist. I saw his duet and I raised him one. I suggested we consider taking our show on the road. I proposed an Eastern European tour in the spring. I told him I had a connection in Latvia. This was true. He said he had one in Lithuania. I felt things were coming together nicely. But before that, as a first step, I proposed we do a show here in New York. I made the invitation on a lark, of course. He responded by saying something like, "It won't surprise you to learn that I am penniless, but my son works for Air France, so it's easy enough for me to hop on a plane."

Suddenly I was faced with the reality of Imre Lodbrog as a houseguest. I shrugged and asked the rhetorical question, "Imre, how bad can you be?" He didn't seem to understand that the question was rhetorical, so he began to answer it, circumspectly. He said something about not telling me where he was in 1992. I hazarded a guess that it was prison. He seemed impressed by my detective skills.

How, you may be wondering, did I get us our first gig? Well, this first one fairly fell into our laps. Two artist friends of mine, Courtney Smith and Ivan Navarro, had been given a residency at a gallery in lower Manhattan, the Hôtel Particulier. They'd opted to curate a series of performances on top of a sculptural installation that Smith would design. It would have several functions in the course of their residency – as an occasional platform for other objects being exhibited and sold in the gallery, as a stage for live performances, and as a table for a madcap, surreal meal that would be orchestrated one evening by a food artist. It was also, of course, a work in its own right, in Smith's vein of raw and yet whimsical, citational carpentry. This sculpture was to be illuminated by Navarro's own sculptural configurations of neon bulbs. For some reason, they thought it might be interesting for me to do something involving my ukulele cover tunes, or possibly the reading of a text, on that platform. When they approached me about the possibility, a little lightbulb went off over my head. Actually, it was more like a very big lightbulb, one of Ivan's massive glowing neon tubes. I said, "I don't suppose you'd be interested in a collaborative performance with my French stalker?" Courtney, being francophone, and also one of my closest friends, was already familiar with "Browning," a song that she – like me – had deemed an instant classic. She and Ivan green-lighted my crackpot scheme, no hesitation.

Of course, their risk was minimal, there being no expense involved (thank you, Air France). In fact, a Chilean *pisco* manufacturer had offered to provide free booze. The only person taking a real gamble was me, offering this Lodbrog character my guest bed. Well, of course it was also pretty reckless of him to accept my invitation, which promised no fiscal compensation whatsoever. That part didn't seem to faze him. He did register a little bewilderment, though it wasn't clear whose welfare concerned him – his or mine. He said, "Are you sure?" I said, "Imre, throw caution to the wind." He seemed to like that phrase. Imre likes English colloquialisms. I later sent him a link to a webpage that gives an astonishing number of slang expressions for female masturbation. He promptly arranged them into the lyrics of a song.

But back to our gig. My idea was to begin the evening with a short literary segment, and then move to a musical performance of some songs we'd been working on together, all of Imre's composition. I like to work right at the border between fiction and nonfiction, and I thought it might be good to factually document the origins of this evidently fictional character who, never the less, was creating real music.

He did, quickly and willingly, offer up his real name, Sébastien Régnier. It took less than a minute to figure out that he was a French *scènariste*, evidently a greater *succès d'éstime* than in the box office. I lied and said that although I'd Googled Lodbrog, if he thought I was going to research Régnier he had another thing coming. I was pretty sure he wouldn't believe me. It was just a minor, friendly retaliation for his own disinclination to figure out who the hell I was.

That's not to say he appeared disinterested – just old-fashioned. He seemed to have accepted that Google, Wikipedia, Twitter, YouTube, Facebook and SoundCloud were perhaps necessary evils in the process of contemporary art making, but if he were giving or getting dirt on his own or somebody else's life history, it seems he wanted it delivered over that bottle of Vouvray, or between hits of weed. That wasn't just a question of style. It was becoming clear that despite his hard-ass photo, Imre was the sensitive type. He liked his reality slightly softened, whether by liquid or smoke. He also mentioned a sweet tooth. I made a mental note of all this. There were a few things I'd obviously need to stock up on in preparation for his visit.

And then there was another whole level of preparation: in the three or four short weeks we had before his arrival, he began assigning me homework – books to read, films to watch, YouTube links to both Franco- and Anglophone songs he thought I should be familiar with. Why the books and films? At first it seemed because they were thematically linked to the compositions he was proposing to me for our repertoire, but pretty soon, when he saw that I was game, it appeared he just wanted to share some things with me that he loved.

The first novel he insisted I read was Victor Hugo's *L'Homme qui rit*. The book was weird – and long. About seven hundred pages. I read it in a few days. It told the story of the love between a disfigured young man and a blind girl. Their protector was an irascible old mountebank with a pet wolf. For a while the young man got sidetracked by a spoiled, seductive duchess who found him fascinating despite, or perhaps because of, his disfigurement. I wondered if this was supposed to be some kind of allegory for us. I asked if I was supposed to identify with the blind girl, the spoiled duchess, or the wolf. Imre said all three. This would seem to suggest that he was an amalgam of the hideously deformed youth and the irascible old traveling huckster.

There was something unusual about the style and tempo of this book. I told Imre, *"j'aime les phrases courtes de hugo."* He answered, *"J'aime les phrases courtes de Hugo et les longs mails de toi."* I love Hugo's short sentences and your long emails. In point of fact, the message he was referring to wasn't long at all, at least for me. I'm a bit notorious for my electronic correspondence, which I sometimes pilfer for my fiction. I wrote back, *"hm, tu trouves ça long?"* – you find that long? – "i'm a monster, imre, one critic called me the d.h. lawrence of the email. i'm not sure if you realize what you've gotten yourself into." This didn't seem to scare him, particularly.

But back to real literature. There was more. Imre wrote me about his love of Cervantes (comparing himself to the hero of his masterpiece – I told him I'd just made this very connection myself in trying to describe him to a friend), and also Calderón's *La vida es sueño*. These I knew well. But there was one other book he insisted I had to read. It was the compiled journals and wartime correspondence of Etty Hillesum, a Jewish woman from the Netherlands who chronicled the German occupation. She was just twenty-nine when she died at Auschwitz. Imre said he deeply loved this book and he'd even gone so far as to join some sort of "Society of the Friends of Etty Hillesum" in order to remain abreast of any activities or publications concerning her. It's true that the book was immensely moving. At first I thought maybe he'd suggested it to me because Hillesum, like me, was something of a sensualist, and prone to passionate defenses of women's sexual independence. I also tend to pontificate on the subject. Of course, given the historical circumstances under which Hillesum was writing, she addressed other questions of freedom as well. But it was impressive how often she came back to the importance of taking pleasure – and not just sexual pleasure, though that was part of it. She also really loved tastes, colors, smells – and people's hands. And art. She could get very passionate about art. Now, on reflection, I can see the absurd vanity of thinking that I had reminded him of Hillesum. The context of horror in which her journals had been written was of an almost unimaginable dimension. Later, when I met Imre's mother, I realized that Etty had probably reminded him of her. She'd passed through that same horror with the same astonishing embrace of life.

In response to Imre's varied bibliographic assignments, I offered him, perhaps solipsistically, a single text: my own first novel. I could make various excuses for this on the basis of resonances with the books I've already mentioned, but the truth is, I wanted Imre to be fully aware of my modus operandi. My book recounted an amorous relationship with an artist, who was somewhat confusingly described at different moments as female, male, Malian, Israeli, 68, and 23.

Well, obviously one person can't be all those things at once, but it amounted to a fairly accurate depiction of my affective and erotic history – and also my approach to narrating the events of my life and those around me. That is, as a writer, I tend to turn "reality" into a self-revealing semi-fiction which I announce as such. I always ask permission if I drag somebody into this process. Since Imre already appeared to be semi-fictional, I thought he might be up for this kind of experiment.

He told me he'd started my book and found it lively, but he had to put it down pretty quickly. It seemed some of the personal revelations were coming at him a little faster and more furiously than he was comfortable with. That was okay. I figured he'd get around to it eventually. I registered his sensitivity in relation to the facts of life.

Actually, when I'd told that friend of mine that Imre reminded me of Don Quixote, I was referring to my impression that he was somebody who was somewhat more comfortable living in a realm of fantastic tales than in what most people would designate the "real world." I wasn't talking about his physical type. And yet when I met him in person, I was struck by his resemblance to the actor Jean Rochefort in Terry Gilliam's famously aborted attempt to make a film version of Cervantes' novel. At other moments he bore an uncanny resemblance to John Neville as he appeared in Gilliam's "Adventures of Baron Munchausen." It perhaps goes without saying that Gilliam would seem to be attracted to a certain type, and Imre fits the bill: dignified, poignant, and a little the worse for wear. Also, like Neville in the role of Munchausen, he's something of a shape-shifter – particularly in regard to his apparent age.

He'd told me about that before we met. I'd seen that photograph of his online, in which his grizzled and craggy qualities were evident, but he was referring to something else. One of his other videos on YouTube cross-faded eerily and fleetingly between images of him shrouded in the regular Lodbrog armor (fedora, rocker shades, leather jacket) and him denuded – no armor at all. His willingness to shed momentary light on his bare pate and naked shoulders made him appear, well, as I just said, dignified, poignant, and a little the worse for wear. But Imre wanted to make absolutely sure I got the picture before he arrived. He wrote me a couple of days before coming, saying that he'd caught a glimpse of himself in a window on a train and he was so struck by his own image that he took a photograph.

He said it wasn't vanity at all that made him take the shot. On the contrary. He thought I should know that he looked pretty worn out, and older than his calendar years. He indicated that the last decade or so had been pretty trying. He didn't say what had happened, but it evidently hadn't been a walk in the park.

He was also pretty clear about his material situation. The Air France freebie situation notwithstanding, Imre was basically skint, ass-out, on stamps. But he said he'd indulged in a little something for his travels. He'd bought a cheap suitcase on wheels at a Chinese import store in Paris – "green, the color of hope." He didn't say what he was hoping for.

Chapter 2
The Birth of a Legend

IMRE LODBROG WAS BORN IN JULY 2008, with a hangover and on the road between Cherbourg and Evreux. He wasn't a newborn babe. He had fifty-six years under his belt.

I was on my way back from seeing Freddy. But was that really Freddy? His enigmatic words the night before, as he'd stared at me with a slight walleyed look, still shook me to the core: "The guy who's speaking to you at this moment, Seb, is not me…" In the course of my visit, Freddy urged me to change my name. Or at least to adopt a new one for the rock 'n' roll adventures that awaited us. A new name? To give birth to a new me? The idea might be interesting, but… What name?

Sometime around the year 800, a more or less mythic Viking king was thrown into a swarming pit of vipers to meet his end: Ragnar Lodbrog. Such a death could only lead to the birth of a legend… My father had the firm conviction that our family name, Régnier, was derived from Ragnar, our Norman origins erasing all doubt.

In another time, somewhere in Transylvania, my mother's father was called Imre. She was two years old when she lost him. According to my mother and a few other rare testimonies, he was a wise man, a patriarch, the solid trunk of a family tree with wide branches – today reduced to almost nothing.

At kilometer 244, the collage came together on its own: Imre Lodbrog. It seemed obvious. The idea that it was practically unpronounceable and hard to remember pleased me in equal proportion. I stepped on the accelerator.

So, my real name is Sébastien Régnier. And for Sébastien Régnier, the twenty-first century had begun well enough. After fifty years of Parisian life, I'd thrown in the towel and moved to the country. With my longtime companion Atika, I had a six-year-old daughter, Lucie. Often, the roles of children and their parents are reversed. The good we want to do them returns to us like a boomerang. At the end of the summer of '99, which is to say at the end of the school holiday, we discover Lucie crying in a corner. We're on vacation in the south of France. When we ask her what's wrong, she tells us, "I don't want to go back to Paris!"

That's the straw that breaks the camel's back. Suddenly I can't even imagine her growing up in the unhealthy gloom of the capital. We promise Lucie that before her next school vacation, we'll be living in the country.

I will always love Paris. But in the past few decades, Paris has changed a lot. The air is charged with an ambient nervousness, and often agressivity. And gone is the time of cheap little pleasures, like sitting at an outdoor café over a coffee, watching the passersby. Life has gotten impossibly expensive. The population has gentrified, and the good old neighborhoods like Belleville or Ménilemont have crumbled like sand castles. When I think of my youth, it's like another city, another epoch, another film.

In June of 2000, we leave Paris for Pourry, a picturesque little hamlet (whose name, ironically, sounds like "rotten" in French), with about two hundred inhabitants, on the edge of a forest. For a pittance, we buy an old Norman country house. The city rat has turned into a country mouse, finally realizing a childhood dream: we have a few chickens, rabbits, cats, ferrets, and a dog. In fact, the king of dogs: we name him Ragnar – as in that Viking myth that already looms over this story.

A period of true happiness. The arc of the sky is 360°, I rediscover the seasons, the ellipse of the sun, the evolution of the moon, everything smells good – the hay in the summer and the wood smoke in the winter. And what's more, however much you may sympathize with Karl Marx, being a property owner isn't nothing. I remember the voluptuous sense of pissing, for the first time, under the stars in MY garden.

One spring morning, in 2002, finally having given in to Atika's insistence, I become a father for the fourth and final time. Anouk arrives. A baby owl we found in the forest comes to complete our bestiary, and it becomes Anouk's guardian angel, perched on the frame of her cradle, scrutinizing with its round eye this strange little creature. As for work, I have nothing to complain about: one film's just come out, and I'm writing another.

But in 2004, the machine goes off its rails. My father dies – in my arms. I seem to box up the shock of an event I've dreaded all my life. One says that great pains are silent. They're also subterranean. They march through our galleries like termites, crumbling our structures as they go. My notion of time has always been a little hazy, maybe because time and I have never truly been friends. Too short, too fast, too... And not enough. But beginning in 2004, and for several years, time really becomes a formless mass in which all my guideposts sink, except for the alternation of the days and the nights. Christmas seems to come back every two months.

What's more, my relationship is on the rocks. After the enchantment of the first few months, disillusionment strikes Atika: isolation, discomfort, the animals that shit all around us, the mud we track in on the soles of our shoes... She misses everything about Paris, the pleasures, her work. Me, I won't budge, and anyway, it's too late. If it was hard to leave Paris, going back is practically impossible. So, I begin to look like some sort of jailer in a confinement I thought we'd chosen together. And finally: no more income is in view: the day arrives when I deposit our last check, The specter of material difficulty returns. I should have been used to it, but this time, it was one time too many.

When I was ten years old, at the Porte de Montreuil, a fucking gypsy grabbed my hand to read my future. After which, she pronounced her prognosis: she traced in the air a chain of mountains, with crests and valleys, highs and lows, explaining: "Your life will be like that!"

She saw right. My life has never had a head or a tail. Blown by the wind here and there, passing from calm to storm, from inertia to chaos, from here to there, from solitude to multitude, from hardship to provisional ease, from high to low and low to high without any precise direction or a clear cause and effect, except for those provoked by pseudo-chance. Everything in the name of a wild and innate dread of an "ordinary life," with La Fontaine's fable "The Dog and the Wolf" as my guiding principle:

> "You live on a leash?," said the wolf. "You don't run free wherever you want?"
> "Not always, but does it matter?"
> "It matters so much…"

Grosso modo, a sort of enslavement to liberty. But having arrived midway between fifty and sixty, I'd suddenly had my fill of, as we say, holding the devil by the tail – being tossed around by fate, on a precarious loop. All that made for a rather bitter brew, and instead of facing the facts, I put my head in the sand.

That year in Pourry after Atika left, the cannabis plants I've been cultivating give a remarkable harvest, supercharged with THC. Enough to fill two garbage bags. I consume them almost all by myself between the fall and the spring. Let's just say it is a smoky winter. Well, smoke and depression make a nice little team: one accelerates the other, which makes one want more. It can seem like you're protecting oneself and when in fact you're drowning. Same goes for alcohol. But the biggest error, without a doubt, was abandoning music, the guitar, my songs. Since the age of fifteen, I'd written more than two thousand songs. Aside from two or three little televised eccentricities, they hadn't done anything for me – and I hadn't done anything for them. That garden had never produced anything but wilted flowers. It was time to hit the brakes. My guitar had been sleeping in its case, and my dreams of music slept with it. As for travels, which had always provided both the tempo and the color of my life, they'd been packed up with the suitcases on the top shelf of my closet. Elsewhere had definitively gone back to being elsewhere.

That's when I begin dragging myself through the gloom, with my little Anouk as a sole ray of sunshine. She accompanies me (along with Ragnar) on my walks in the forest whatever the weather. "Storms give you courage!" was one of her first sentences. I occupied myself with the construction of a little tent in which we spent some enchanted nights.

But each morning becomes an ever murkier swamp to cross. What good is it putting one foot in front of the other, letting the days add up? After all, I tell myself, maybe I've had my run. My life has been rich in all kinds of experiences, dense in extravagances, just like I've wanted it, at the cost of any strategy for security, and I hardly wanted to vegetate my way to the cemetery. What can I hope for now? A new life, a new love, new travels, a resurrection? Reality is right there in the mirror, where my face is turning into a crumpled dishrag. I was seeing the face of my grandfather looking at me.

A little parenthesis: over there, wherever he is, my father keeps sending me signs. In life, he had a habit of writing down phrases, thoughts, quotations, on little scraps of paper that he left here and there among the pages of his books. Since he left, I've often found these bits of paper. One of those sad mornings in Pourry, I find the following words in his hand, seemingly posed there in the night, a quotation from Bergson:

"The future is there. It calls us, or rather pulls us toward it. That uninterrupted traction that makes us advance down our path is also a continual cause of our action."

A motor to the future? It left me thinking…

One day, Danielle, a dear old friend, sees me and says, "Have you looked at yourself in the mirror lately?!" She presses me to get some treatment for depression ASAP. She's been through that herself… A shrink confirms it. Insomniac, undernourished, I've waited far too long, it seems, and my condition is diagnosed as Major Depression.

Me? Depressed? Impossible! I had so many friends who had suffered from that condition, some to the point of ending it all, and I'd always tried to support them as best I could, thinking myself invincible. The confirmation of the diagnosis, with a big old prescription for antidepressants to boot, just makes me more depressed. With Atika, this really announces the beginning of the end. Mired in my own descent, I'm barely balancing on a high wire stretched over an abyss.

Our social universe doesn't help much. In our world of winners, it's no good to lose. So it's a sublime irony that, a few years later, the kind of losers extends his hand. Frédérique Tchékovitch, AKA Freddy.

Coming back from his place in Cherbourg, in 2008, I took his advice and created this salutary schizophrenia. There would be, on the one side, Sébastien Régnier, screenwriter on the decline, and on the other, Imre Lodbrog, a newborn phantom to whom I'd give body and soul. A sort of liberation. As if a pseudonym would be enough. As if changing names were the same as changing skins.

Thanks to Freddy, I take my guitars out of their cases and get back to work on my songs – but this time the tone has changed. No more sad little balads: I have The Stones in my head and I'm spitting venom. My voice has also changed. And my look. In short, I've molted. As Lodbrog now, I would turn my black years into electric fuel.

My old friend Gregory, intrigued by this Lodbrog concept, makes a couple video clips where my clone appears on YouTube in his war gear: a Stetson, a pair of dark glasses, and a sullen mug. A while later, around the beginning of 2013, I think, this same Gregory suggests that I put my songs on SoundCloud, a site with an aerian name where musicians from all over the world – mostly amateurs – post their work just for the pleasure of sharing it. After a few weeks, I find myself with about a dozen "followers." Pretty quickly, I pass from twelve to fifty, a hundred, a hundred and fifty… Somebody's listening to me on all five continents. A new form of anonymity, but also, a sort of pleasing form of recognition.

I've always frequented record stores, kept up on what was coming out—an addicted musicophage— until the stores all started closing. Now, on SoundCloud,

I rediscover the pleasure of discovery. Some real artists are hiding out there, one just has to look for them in the hodgepodge, from electronica to the blues, from pseudo-classical to rock ... One day, I stumble on a little piece, I forget the title – but it hooks me right away. A feminine voice, a ukulele – and that's it.

A name like a gunshot: Barbara Browning.

I love it, so I "like" it, and I leave a little comment. Then I visit her page, with hundreds of covers, all in the same minimalist style. I always loved miniatures.

7 January, 2014 – I haven't forgotten the date. What happens? I'm just about to catch the train to Paris when a strange fly bites me. I grab my guitar, three chords, a little reggae rhythm, and the words, like the music, come to me on their own.

The music is light, the words less so:

Cette fille est un killer
Et moi j'ignore encore
À quoi le destin me destine.
Mais si je meure avant l'heure,
La tête, le coeur, le corps,
Oh! Que ce soit d'un coup de Browning.
Barbara Browning.
Barbara Browning.

That girl's a killer, and me, I still don't know where destiny's leading me. But if I die before my time, head, heart, body, let it be of a shot from a Browning... The title of the song? "Barbara Browning." I just have enough time to record it and post it on SoundCloud before I catch my train.

Once I'm on board, I bite my fingers. Such a personal song, with the name of a stranger for a title, that's a bit presumptuous, no? What if she sues me? Americans love to sue, and Barbara's American. Getting off the train at Saint-Lazare, I just have one thing in mind, to plug my computer in and correct the error by taking down the song. But the dice are already cast: the first comments and "like"s have already appeared, so I content myself with rebaptising the tune, removing her first name. After all, a Browning is a fairly ordinary object. And then I forget about it.

Until the next day. Not only does it seem that Barbara Browning doesn't intend to sue me, but she's even sent a response, tit for tat, as it were, in the form of a cover of one of my songs: *"Tu veux de l'or."* You want gold. Direct hit. A few private messages follow. Something's taking shape. I take a closer look at her page. Identifying factors – a photo, the name of a city, and a short text. The photo: head cut off, and the sketch of a body in a knowing penumbra – it looks to me like a girl who could be one of my daughters. The city: New York. As for the text, it's just a few lines followed by "see more…" – but I read the snippet quickly and don't want to know more.

In one of her first messages, she throws me a question: "Who made you up?"

That strikes me. Me, I know the answer, but it can't be explained in a short online message, and how can I plunge via email into a story that's taken place across forty years? I leave it at this: "It would take a fireplace and a good bottle of Vouvray to tell you that…"

Meanwhile, I propose to Barbara that we record

a long-distance duet, with a certain intuition that our voices would go nicely together. The assonance of "Browning / Lodbrog" encourages me. She says okay:

> if you send me an mp3 and some words, i'll sing wherever you tell me to, whatever you tell me to. then i'll send you an mp3 of my naked voice, and you can mix it in however you like. if you insist, i'll send my track "dry," which in english means with no reverb whatsoever. that's not particularly flattering. the gentlemanly thing to do is to allow a woman to send her voice at least a little wet. :)

That last bit sounds a little naughty, so, all right, I'll be a gentleman. The theme of "Beauty and the Beast" occurs to me. Parodying the famous song from *West Side Story*, on the train from Paris to Evreux, I mentally birth a waltz in Franglais, "I Feel Ugly," in which, in alternating phrases, one loses track of just who is ugly and who is pretty. I record it, and send it along with the lyrics typed in red for her, blue for me. A few days later, the song is posted on SoundCloud and is received as a frank success by our followers. That encourages me to dive into another duet: "Down and Up." Then comes "Naked Lady with a Ukulele," and some others... It's February, and we practically have a repertoire already. One day she asks me to do a cover of Gainsbourg's "Initials BB." I whip it off right away, and from that moment on I take to calling her "Bébé".

That's when Bébé advances a pawn on our little chessboard. "I don't suppose," she asks in the negative interrogative, "that you could get to New York next month?" She could organize a concert for us on 15 March.

She doesn't know about the joker up my sleeve. I tell her, "You suppose wrong." My son Tom works for Air France. As his father, I have the right to five roundtrip tickets per year to any location they fly, for a nominal service fee. Bébé doesn't seem displeased. She presses me to get my ticket: "vas-y, imre, buy your damn ticket, throw caution to the wind." I love this phrase. I obey and reserve my place on a flight on the twelfth of March.

From that point on, the scales are tipping toward the improbable. I begin to think I'm dreaming, and to fear I might wake up, branded as I am by Calderón's play, *La vida es sueño*, in which the hero is yanked from the damp straw of his dungeon only to find himself flung upon a throne – before being tossed once again back into his dungeon.

All that mixes in my head like a slightly troubling cocktail. A few signs of disorder appear. When it takes a while for Bébé to answer an email, my nervousness gets the best of me. That old feeling of being on a high wire. And what if all that were just a joke, a passing fancy of a few days, a flash in the pan? What can one know, in fact, about these millions of Internauts, in their exchanges where nothing actually connects to anything, since one's knowledge of the other is 99% virtual? But the messages keep coming, and Bébé appears to be steadfast, gently setting my worries to rest. Then, just to feed my anxiety, I start to invent other possible problems: a surprise strike by the employees of Air France – or the outbreak of World War III (which doesn't even need to break

26

out; the world is already unraveling daily).

But finally, on 12 March 2014, I find myself nicely set up, ready for boarding at Roissy Airport. Tom's arranged everything, alerting the crew to my presence on the flight. I'm led like a VIP to the upper deck of the A380, where I'm placed in a business class seat, the first glass of champagne in my hand. I lift it, in my mind, to Freddy. When the plane takes off, I'm already on my third glass, and I'm flying.

Where am I going? Toward what? New York! One of the great loves of my life. From my first visit there in the '70s to the last in '98. Something of an obsession. I didn't think I'd ever get back there.

And Barbara Browning? A few hours before meeting her, I go over what I know of her, which is the sum of what she wanted or judged necessary for me to know, since I'm an adamant anti-Googler. I know that she's a musician, and a professor at NYU. I also know that she is a dancer, and that is no small part of what I know of her. I've always had a problem with dance. When it wants to make us forget the laws of gravity and our physical weight, it does nothing, to my eyes, other than to remind us of it. Attempts at flight which always evoke for me the "Albatross" of Baudelaire. But I adore Fred Astaire, Michael Jackson, Farid Chopel… And I love Barbara Browning.

She'd sent me the links to her YouTube dance videos. As with her covers, we were dealing with minimalist miniatures. The first of these videos was called "Celebrate the Body Electric." Over a soundtrack of piercing electric guitar, a young man with a naked torso enters the frame and begins to flail. He's soon joined by a girl, and the two go wild, reaching a state of trance, the girl flipping her hair around like a madwoman. The girl? Bébé. The young man? Her son. They could've been a young couple on Ecstasy; it was completely uplifting. In another clip, to one of Satie's *Gnossiennes*, it's a ballerina who uses her body like a marionette, articulating and disarticulating her moves at the ends of invisible strings with a Chaplinesque air. And last, my favorite, her "iPod Samba." Just a woman dancing in her room with her headphones on, in jeans and sneakers... And smiling as she does.

Finally, I know she is a novelist.

I've always found that the books that one loves can be the best way of presenting oneself. I was still under the shock of *L'Homme qui rit*, which I'd discovered late. I'd recommended Hugo's novel to her, which she devoured in a few days. In exchange, she had mailed me her first novel, *The Correspondence Artist*, into which I'd plunged, imagining it to be a work of pure fiction. I was immediately hooked by the liveliness of her voice, her finesse, the mix of humor and emotion – but I was also intrigued and a bit disconcerted by its form. Written in the first person, it seemed to have the scent of an autobiographical account, fed from life with a sense of detail that, as we say, doesn't fool anybody.

Suddenly, it seems like I'm entering the intimate universe of a stranger, one that I'm only beginning to know, and in spite of the pleasurable reading, that's disconcerting. The book exhibited, unvarnished, sexual relations of all kinds, ranging from a young male lover to an older mistress, from Israel to New York passing through Mali in an expanse of raw details, making of the reader an eyewitness – even an involuntary voyeur. I had some difficulty untangling the skein. Fiction, or an intimate journal? I know Bamako well. In the middle of a chapter in which the author finds herself there, I rediscover not only the perfumes and colors but also the precise topography of the place. And I asked myself who could be this "Djeli," the famous musician that she went to meet there, and who had an aversion to oral sex… All of it read like irrefutable lived experience.

But actually, I'd penetrated a literary genre previously unknown to me. Neither real nor fictional, half-real, half-fiction: fictionalization of the real. And Bamako? Bébé had never set foot there! As for her amorous confessions, I'd soon learn that that apparent multiplicity of liaisons could be reduced to a single one, and a bit in the style of Chateaubriand's *Sylphide*, she had fabricated a sort of collage of fictional personae as the portrait of one person, entirely real. Each time I dived into this tissue of confidences, especially on the sexual level, and in spite of my delectation in the text, I quickly ended up asking myself: Do I really want to know all this right now? Wouldn't I rather hold on to that smoky halo through which the image of the Other would reveal itself in its own time, if at all?

I was hoping to tell my backstory in little bits, over time, on long walks through the streets of New York… Or maybe not telling it at all. In short, mystery seemed to me the more appealing option, and I'm ashamed to say that I left my reading in mid-course. Not without promising myself that I'd take it up again one day.

I should mention her inscription: "To Imre, who could have been a character in this book, and surely will be in one to come…"

And one other detail, because she'd said it more than once: Bébé was a feminist. Why had she insisted on this point?

So, there I am, on the upper deck of that Airbus A380, seat number 72 (the year of my first visit to New York), and that's more or less what I know of Barbara Browning. A few hours later, after I've downed a few drinks and watched, yet again, with great pleasure, Godard's *Breathless*, the voice of the flight attendant announces: "We're beginning our descent to John F. Kennedy Airport. Please fasten your seat belts. The ground temperature is…"

I pinch myself. It hurts. That's a good sign.

Chapter 3
Imre Lodbrog Takes Manhattan

WHEN THE DAY CAME, I took the subway to meet Imre at JFK. I was a little nervous – not because of any of this business about his wear and tear, of course, and not even because of that "passé criminel," but because I knew I'd be shy to speak French with him in person. My written French isn't bad, and I can read pretty much everything, but I have a block for speaking. Singing's fine if I have the lyrics in front of me. But regular conversation for me is torture. I get into an exaggerated panic about prepositions.

I did my doctorate in comparative literature, and I wrote a dissertation on French ethnographers of Brazil. Perhaps you know this: there was a relatively short-lived French colony on an island in Guanabara Bay in the sixteenth century called *la France Antarctique*. Obviously, that didn't mean "antarctic" in the sense we use the word today – it basically just meant that the French thought of this colony as an upside-down version of their own country on the flip side of the world. The colonists wrote some highly figurative and evocative things about both the supposed nobility and savagery of the indigenous people, all of which were quite clearly projections of their own image, flipped. These kinds of writings have served at various historical moments and in various parts of the world both to justify and to decry the violences of colonization. Well. As I said, this colony was short-lived. It was established in 1555, was briefly held by the Huguenots, and was demolished by the Portuguese in 1567 – twelve little years if you count them. But it produced some astonishing writings, including those of Jean de Léry, whose *Histoire d'un voyage faict en la terre du Brésil* informed Montaigne's famous essay on cannibalism, which in turn was a source for Shakespeare's *Tempest*. Three and a half centuries later, Claude Levi-Strauss carried a copy of Léry's text in his pocket when he traveled by boat to Brazil, ostensibly to perform ethnographic fieldwork, but more practically, as a Jew, to get the hell out of France during the occupation.

Speaking of which, Imre recently showed me his mother's copy of *Tristes Tropiques*, warmly inscribed to her by Lévi-Strauss himself. Both she and Imre's father had, like me, been academicians. More about that later.

Anyway, I was telling you all this in order to explain something about my French. I spent a lot of time reading it during my studies, and I'm pretty adept at plowing through the weird orthography of the sixteenth century, which Imre says baffles your ordinary contemporary French citizen. I've also read a ton of things that came since, and it may not surprise you that I have an abiding interest in the movements of surrealism and the *nouveau roman*. All of that is well and good, and in addition I've spent a bit of time in the country myself. I lived for a few months in a tiny studio in the Latin Quarter in '88, when I was writing my dissertation, and I took my son to stay in the Marais for another couple of months during a sabbatical twenty years later. But somehow conversational French has always eluded me – unlike Portuguese, which I picked up with almost uncanny ease during my sporadic stays in Brazil.

But my nerves when I was picking up Imre at the airport weren't only about my French. There was another problem: the music. I really hadn't practiced sufficiently for our gig. Imre was arriving just three days before the show. We still had some practical errands to run. We needed to pick up a loaner guitar from my friend Mamie Minch in Brooklyn. Mamie is, I think I can say without much exaggeration, a national treasure. She's a very skilled performer of a traditional blues repertoire. Her fingerpicking is assured and nimble, her voice deep and sensual, her capacity to convey the story in a song utterly captivating. She's physically captivating, too: nearly six feet tall and built, as a blueswoman would say, for comfort, with a charming, Kewpie doll face crowned with black ringlets. The first time I saw her play, I almost fell over.

She's also a professional luthier, and she runs a workshop with a fiddler, Chloe, in Brooklyn. Imre had told me he was accustomed to playing his old Martin acoustic, but was worried about checking it on the plane. He asked me if I might be able to arrange something for him to play on. I asked Mamie if she had a guitar we could rent, but she said she'd be happy to lend us a slightly banged up vintage number she had that she thought might do the trick. I trusted Mamie's instincts. I told Imre, "Travel light." He asked, *"Les mains dans les poches?"* I said yes. Your hands in your pockets.

In addition to the guitar, we also had to pick up some vinyl EPs I was having pressed. That was my cockamamie idea. The obvious thing, of course, would be to make a CD to sell or distribute at the gig. In fact, even a CD was starting to seem like an anachronism, since most everyone now downloads his or her music, whether purchased or pirated, from the Internet. I briefly researched the option of biodegradable download cards embedded with wildflower seeds. I still like that idea. But I had a feeling Imre might get more excited by the idea of moving backwards, rather than forwards, technologically speaking. Well, I got that right. When I suggested a vinyl EP, he fairly flipped. He went off about his adolescent years scavenging for bootlegs and other rarities in record stores. He told me about his extensive early Beatles collection – dormant now for years, as he hadn't had a working turntable in God knows how long – but swaddled lovingly in some corner of his "capharnaüm" – a word I had to look up. It's a high-falutin' term for a pigsty. That's Imre's workspace. He *loved* the idea of having a record pressed. He wondered about the practicality, and the expense, but I told him to leave pragmatic questions to me. I may not be pragmatic in the usual sense of the word, but I have a peculiar talent for making impractical plans work out very practically.

So, between seeing to our equipment and our merch, we had a bit of running around to do, and I was worried that when we finally got down to practicing our set he'd find me sadly lacking. Imre had expressed his own concern on the topic. As I mentioned, even before proposing the New York gig, I'd floated the idea of an international tour. I had a few ideas. That one about Eastern Europe, or maybe a shopping mall in

Abu Dhabi. I also knew somebody there. Imre perked up considerably when I mentioned potential travels, but was wary of the actual stage performance part of the scheme. He wrote me in French, "You may find it a paradox, my hesitation to get on stage, given my enthusiasm about a tour. It's just that it's been a very long time, and if I put that in my head, I realize I need to prepare, technically. And suddenly March seems very soon. But I can buckle down…"

The next day he continued in English:

Do you really mean it for me in March in NY? Watch out! I'm at the edge of taking it seriously and being seriously tempted… But the thing I must confess, is that I turned down all offers to climb on any stage, unless it's a level under the audience. Why? I don't know. Last time I produced myself in public was in 73 if I remember well. Since I developed an incurable shyness, and also I don't know any of my songs. If I want to sing them to myself, I need to put my glasses on and open my big cahier, which is not very sexy. Anyway, we could do something around music. Our little waltz is encouraging as it appears. And we could talk face to face, making huge plans for a major tour in Minor Asia. Per chance to dream.

The waltz in question was that Beauty and the Beast ditty we'd recently recorded together. It was generating some positive commentary from our followers.

I answered:

Imre, I'm relieved to know you only perform in the cellar. (Tu connais "Seedbed" de Vito Acconci?) Me too! I'm totally incompetent on my instrument and I need reading glasses and a notebook full of words. But it's okay, I've convinced these curators that I'm a conceptual artist – you can hitch a ride on my scam! Besides, they're not paying us... You should definitely come. March 5, or 4 if you arrive in the evening. Stay 5 days or so on my guest bed, with the proviso that I kick you out briefly on a daily basis. After that you can crash with somebody else if you want. I am dead serious about the tour.

I explained that I thought a tour could make interesting fodder for a book I might write.

Un film documentaire serait plus évident qu'un roman, mais je suis romancière. I already said thank you for the Hugo. You can make the film if you want. Then we'll be tit for tat, as the saying goes.

He knew the expression. He said he'd had some experience with documentary film.

Well. There we had it. Depending on how you looked at it, we might be two seasoned writers reasonably colluding to document a fairly unique artistic phenomenon, or we might be a couple of aging, shy hucksters making ill-advised plans to expose our musical – and physical – foibles.

Maybe these possibilities were not mutually exclusive.

I was standing at the exit of his gate at JFK. I was holding my Lanikai soprano ukulele. I'd brought the uke for three strategic reasons: so he'd recognize me right away, so I could practice a little while waiting at the gate, and so I'd have something to do on the train on the way back to Manhattan if the conversation faltered. I got there right on time, and plucked meekly on the little nylon strings while I watched the arrivals board that indicated he'd already touched down. Slowly, the Air France passengers began to emerge: sleek business-suited guys with stylish glasses, a regal West African woman in a boubou, a redhead who looked like a fashion model… And then there he was, unmistakably Imre. His head was dipped down a little, but he was looking directly at me, with just a hint of a smile. He was wearing the Stetson hat that I knew from his photo. He was dragging that cheap Chinese suitcase, awkwardly, as one of the wheels had already fallen off. The zipper was also coming apart at the seams. He passed through the gate and we faced each other. It was true. He seemed more spirit than flesh. He looked and smelled like parchment. I had the sense that if I blew on him he might be lofted up like a feather. But when we embraced, his arms were surprisingly strong. We held onto each other for quite a few seconds.

Imre was a little shorter than I'd imagined – bigger than me, but not by a lot.

We exchanged a few words about his flight. His English was good but a bit faltering, more due to nerves, it seemed, than anything else. His speaking voice was very quiet and I had to lean in to hear him. I said, "This way, Imre," and led him toward the AirTrain.

On the way home, we went through several of our tunes, singing softly so as not to aggravate our fellow passengers. Well, later it would become clear that our signature sound would invariably be on the soft side – but on the train we were particularly muted. I plinked on the chords when I knew them. We both choked on some of the lyrics, but reassured each other that all we needed was a bit more practice. We were mid-route to my house when we tacitly agreed to give it a break. I held the uke in my lap and put my head on Imre's shoulder. It felt like the thing to do. He didn't seem to mind.

How to explain the strangely comfortable rapport between two total strangers? Of course we'd exchanged a certain amount of personal information in our correspondence before his arrival. I'm not a particularly shy person, though I tend toward reticence. Imre's timid, but I didn't feel him to be uneasy with me. He seemed, rather, to be a little stunned by the circumstances he found himself in. It was sort of like watching a man observing himself in a dream. I decided to take him by the hand and bash ahead.

The next 48 hours went by in a flurry – the days spent trekking out to industrial strips of Brooklyn, retrieving equipment and cases of vinyl. I'd kind of impulsively and impractically had those EPs pressed at Brooklyn Phono. I had an idea that we could sell them at our gig, but with an unusual twist. We would offer three payment options: one note of US currency of any denomination ($1, $5, $10, $20, $100…); one object of comparable aesthetic value; or one object of comparable sentimental value. This would put the burden of establishing value (of whatever kind) on the purchaser. I thought that might be an interesting exercise for people. Also, they could consider their own resources, and give us whatever they felt they had to offer.

By now, you will have surmised that my economic philosophy could basically be reduced to: From each, according to her ability; to each, according to her need. I had made the initial financial investment, since I was the one with a steady teaching gig. Imre had obviously done the lion's share of the artistic labor, having written all our songs. I suggested that whatever we sold at the gig we could split, and then I'd give him the leftover records to take back to France, where he could sell them under less or more cock-eyed conditions as he saw fit, or he could just try to palm them off on friends. I also suggested that we give a short stack to Smith and Navarro, and another to the owner of the gallery, to do with as they wished.

This struck Imre as more than equitable. He later told me that, given his constitutional incapacities with the nuts and bolts of having an artistic career, he'd gladly contract a willing and able manager for a 90/10 split – with the manager receiving the 90%. This went for his writing as well as his music. I'm still not sure if it was good or catastrophic luck on Imre's part that I got this bee in my bonnet about getting him on stage. An outside observer might find the deal I was offering him at best weird, and at worst, possibly abusive. In truth, I was anything but predatory. But if our haul was mostly constituted of objects of sentimental value, well, Imre hardly has a shortage of those. He could use a little cash money.

The proprietor of the gallery where we'd be playing, the Hôtel Particulier, is an elegant Frenchwoman named Frederique Thiollet. She tends to dress in well-tailored, masculine clothes. When Courtney introduced me to her, I tried to describe, in brief, our planned performance. I gave her a line about Imre being like Serge Gainsbourg on 'shrooms, but she smiled and said, "But Serge Gainsbourg was already like Serge Gainsbourg on 'shrooms," which I guess is kind of true.

Anyway, as I said, our first couple of days involved a lot of running around, but the evenings were dedicated to practicing. The initial night perhaps should have been disheartening. We really did need our reading glasses, and there was a fair amount of fumbling on both our parts. But I felt so encouraged that our level of awkwardness was comparable, and he seemed to have infinite patience, which was a big relief. After struggling through the set list a couple of times, we rewarded ourselves with shots of Jim Beam (he'd brought his own supply) and Imre smoked a bit of the weed I'd procured on his behalf. The next night, we were starting to sound almost plausible. We'd cautiously eye each other after we'd nailed a tune. I think each of us was waiting for the other to call his or her bluff, but in fact, we were both surprising ourselves with our increasing competence.

On the day of the show, our hired guns came a couple of hours before our scheduled start-up time to do a run-through. I had thought it might be good to have a little back-up, so I'd asked Imre what he thought of having a cellist and a drummer join us. He liked the idea. The cellist was a really lovely graduate student of mine named Ethan. I was familiar with his own quirky repertoire, and knew him to be a nimble improviser, and also somebody who might pick up on Imre's distinctive charm. He, in turn, suggested the drummer, a gentle, unflappable guy who had worked with some other oddball outfits. Being actual working musicians, the two of them quickly found their bearings, and I think Imre and I were emboldened by the fact that they seemed to think we knew what we were doing. They smiled and nodded encouragingly as we worked our way through the set. If it was a gag, we went along with it. When it was time to head over to the gallery, Imre pocketed his little stash of Jim Beam, and we walked out the door.

The soundcheck went smoothly enough. We fit comfortably on the stage, which resembled a Viking ship carved out of raw pine. It seems Courtney had been at least in part inspired by the Lodbrog legend. Imre took this in with a kind of subdued wonder. There was about an hour to kill before people would start arriving. I began arranging our vinyls and a couple of other items of merch on a side table. I'd brought a few copies of my books, which I was hawking under similar terms to those of our EPs. Courtney had set up some tiny screens in the bathroom where a few of my dance videos were playing on a loop. These videos were related to another writing project. Depending on your perspective, they might be described as lyrical and uncanny, or baffling and mildly obscene. Imre later told me he didn't see them. I guess he didn't have to pee.

While we were still setting things up, I kept Imre

in the corner of my eye. He wandered off for a few minutes and returned with a can of Budweiser in a paper bag. It looked to me like he'd killed the Jim Beam. But when I asked him how he was feeling he didn't seem to be too hammered.

A couple of days before Imre's arrival, there had been another performance in the space, on the same stage where we'd be playing, and I'd gone to see it. Ivan and two other guys made droning electronic music with what only appeared to be complete disregard for the audience members. These, for their part, looked on in rapt attention, many photographing or filming an odd blob wrapped in black plastic at the center of the stage. There was a high-def video camera focused on a rip in the plastic sheath, through which could be seen a human ear. The image of this ear was being projected on a screen above the stage.[1] The performance climaxed when Ivan took a very sensitive microphone and aimed it at this ear while dropping, with a medical dropper, tiny amounts of hydrogen peroxide into the wrapped guy's ear. The enormous projection showed foam extruding from the ear, while the sensitive mic amplified a strange, rumbling, volcanic sound throughout the space. When it was over, the guy crawled out of the black plastic bag and took a bow. Everybody seemed to like it. I wasn't

[1] The ear in question belonged to Diego Fernandez, another Chilean artist who once gamely appeared in a YouTube video as a fictional character of mine. That is to say, he's the kind of friendly person who will do most anything if you ask him. Courtney later told me that Ivan asked him to play this particular role as he's a big, rather hirsute person, seemingly suited for such a ritual of abjection, but when they actually projected the image, hi-def and enormously magnified, on the screen, they realized that Diego had small, remarkably beautiful, hairless, perfect ears.

sure what this indicated in regard to our upcoming show. I did tell Imre that our microphones would be sensitive. He was a little worried since, as I mentioned, neither of us is what you'd call a belter.

The crowd was pretty sizable for that foaming ear show, but on the night of our gig, the house was jam-packed. In advance of Imre's arrival, I'd created an invitation, and I'd circulated it as widely as I could. I felt that Imre, being the composer and carrying most of the musical responsibility, should take top billing. In fact, I preferred not to use my name at all. I suggested we call our act *"Imre Lodbrog et sa Petite Amie."* He liked the sound of that, but seemed mystified by, or maybe curious about, the possible implications. I reminded him that this *petite amie* bit was a stage persona – as, for that matter, was Imre Lodbrog. He shrugged his assent.

I'd actually spent quite a bit of time poking around on Google to fully grasp, myself, the implications of the expression. I wanted it to be suggestive, but slightly ridiculous. I also liked the idea of effacing myself, knowing that in fact, Imre was, as I've pointed out, taking considerable risk by putting himself in the palm of my hand. I knew I was nice, but how could he be sure? This belittling sub-moniker seemed to me emblematic of both my innocence and my possible monstrosity.

"Little friend" is also a euphemism in English, and one I've sometimes used with a similar sense of irony. In my personal life, I also occasionally use the term "special friend." *Petite amie* – or *petit ami* in the masculine – is used by the French a little more commonly in the regular old way that people say "girlfriend" or "boyfriend" in English. But if you ask me, those terms are already pretty ridiculous when applied to anybody over the age of twelve. I've long had an aversion to the usual terms people use to refer to their lovers – except for that term itself, lover. Don't get me started on "partner." Somehow I thought Imre would understand all that without me having to explain it. Obviously, our partnership at this point was strictly musical.

So, we had a title for our act, but what would be the image? I had a nice, slightly racy photo of myself from the waist down, in a tutu. I'd taken it as a possible cover image for my last novel, but my publisher worried it was too dirty for the window display at Barnes & Noble. I thought maybe I could make use of it now. But what about an image of Imre? His online photo seemed too straightforward. I did a Google Image search of "satyr." Bingo. A beautiful drawing popped right up, Michelangelo, in just the same ocher hues as my photo, and with just the right balance of suggestiveness and anguish. Here's what I came up with:

WHO THE HELL IS IMRE LODBROG?

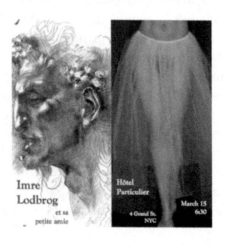

Imre
Lodbrog
et sa
petite amie

Hôtel
Particulier

4 Grand St.
NYC

March 15
6:30

Who the hell is Imre Lodbrog?

There's a pithy description I use to describe him to friends: "He's like Serge Gainsbourg on shrooms."

But if I were to be a little less cheeky, and if I were to elaborate, I'd tell you what I once told Imre in an email. I said, "I was thinking about the appeal of our music and I think it's that you sound like an actor playing the role of an aging rock star, which is precisely the appeal of Leonard Cohen and Bob Dylan, not to mention Frank Sinatra and Léo Ferré..."

...

In this evening of music, video installation and reading, Barbara Browning will introduce Imre Lodbrog, an aging French rock star and minor - or possibly major - genius. Barbara Browning writes fiction, and Imre Lodbrog is fictional, but she didn't make him up. Imre Lodbrog did it for her, and served himself up on a platter. Barbara Browning invited him to come from Paris to New York so she could eat him whole. In return, she offered herself as his muse, back-up singer, and "little friend." This is their performance debut. The will also be releasing their 7" vinyl EP, with accompanying digital disc, Imre Lodbrog et sa petite amie.

I wondered, of course, what Imre would make of the line about serving himself up on a platter. He didn't seem to mind. It was only after he came to New York that I realized how astonishing the resemblance was between him and this drawing by Michelangelo.

I'm not sure if this invitation had anything to do with it, or if it was me or Courtney and Ivan or Frederique who managed to dig up this crowd, but when our announced start-up time arrived, there wasn't a lot of wiggle-room in the house. The space was quite large, open and airy, but it was filled to capacity with bodies. In fact, it was a strikingly attractive crowd. We later learned that that Chilean *pisco* manufacturer used footage from the event to make a commercial, and in it,

Imre and I appear to be minor celebrities.

So, that night, at 7 p.m. sharp, an assistant dimmed the lights and began projecting the video of the ostensible "Lodbrog Bros." At its conclusion, I mounted the stage and asked the wide-eyed crowd, "Who the hell is Imre Lodbrog?" Obviously, they must have been asking themselves the same question. While he lurked on the sidelines, I gave the audience twenty minutes or so of speculation and innuendo, peppered with improbable and yet true references to various trans-Atlantic, Baltic and Indian Oceanic plots and exploits. Just when I felt I had everyone really confused, I called Imre and our hired guns up to the stage. Imre took his sweet time to meander up there, but once everyone was in place, astonishingly, we banged out our set virtually without a hitch. People applauded between numbers, but as Imre sang, they were completely silent, and immobile. What were they thinking? It's possible they were bewildered or befuddled. But I think they may just have found him entrancing.

When we came to the last number, I explained that I was going to leave the stage, and that they'd understand why when they heard the song. It was "Browning." When he finished singing, Imre looked up shyly at his clapping public and when they quieted down, he fumbled in his pocket for a second, pulled out a small camera, and asked if he could take their picture.

Everybody smiled.

IMRE STAYED A FEW MORE DAYS. As threatened, I kicked him out on occasion, being a person accustomed to a certain amount of private time. He didn't appear to be offended, and he seemed to like strolling around on his own. But even when he was in the house, he had the capacity to make himself semi-transparent.

Though he hadn't been to New York in quite some time, he had some old friends right in the neighborhood. In fact, the very day he arrived, we were walking down the sidewalk behind my apartment building when we ran into a stunning young woman who embraced him warmly, saying, "Sébastien! How long are you in New York?!" When she parted, he explained that she was the daughter of one of his oldest friends, Joelle, an artist who lived just a few blocks away. They'd met in the Canary Islands in the early '70s, when they were both globetrotting hippies. Imre had had a love affair with her best friend, Rosie, who'd since passed away. After they met, Sébastien continued trekking afround Africa, while Joelle and Rosie, carrying a letter for his parents, went to visit them in Paris. Joelle ended up maintaining a long and rich correspondence with Imre's father, with whom she shared a passion for philosophical reflection. For years, whenever he'd come to New York, Imre had nearly always stayed with Joelle and her husband George, a very affable and intellectually curious lawyer.

So between his solitary walks, that mysterious disappearing act of his, and a visit or two with his friends, Imre made himself fairly scarce during the day. In the evenings, though, we'd go out on the balcony together, and he'd roll himself a cigarette, and we'd talk. I told him a little about my writing. As I said, I'd sent him my first novel, but he'd stopped just part way in – not, he claimed, for lack of interest, but out of something you might call discretion, or possibly a penchant for mystery. So, I didn't want to insist if he didn't feel quite ready to read my fiction, but I did tell him a bit about the French writers that had profoundly influenced me, both stylistically and philosophically. When I mentioned Roland Barthes, Imre said that he'd in fact been a friend of his parents, and that he remembered lying, as a child, under the dining room table, listening to them all talk. Barthes inscribed a book to him, *"Pour Sébastien – pour plus tard… ou pour jamais – mais toujours avec l'amitié de – R. Barthes. Janv 68."* For Sébastien – for later… or for never – but always with the friendship of – R. Barthes. In fact, Imre did later read that book, and he and Barthes ended up meeting a few times for informal, friendly conversations.

On another occasion, Sébastien and his parents had run into Barthes's mother and his parents reintroduced them, saying, "The last time you saw him he was just a toddler! Surely you won't remember…" and she said, "Ah, but those eyes one doesn't forget!" It's true. I'm not sure if they're bird-like, or lizard-like. They're intensely green, and seemingly unblinking. Imre has an affinity for birds, but perhaps even more so for amphibians. In fact, the second and third toes on both of his feet are webbed. You may think I'm joking, but it's true.

We also talked about our families. Sébastien is a very devoted son and father. When he's here, he calls his mother every day to check in on her, and he affectionately addresses her as "Petite," little one. He has two sons from his first relationship and two daughters from the second. He has warm feelings toward both his exes, and they seem to be reciprocated. He told me about his kids, each of whom he loves with a very particular intensity.

He told me one story about his older daughter, Lucie, who had, as a small child, a lazy eye. In fact, my son also did, although it resolved by itself. In Lucie's case, it required a medical intervention, which meant that for a time she had to wear a patch over the stronger eye, in order to strengthen the weaker one. She was given a flesh-colored adhesive patch which had to be affixed to her eye every day. Removing the patch before bedtime was a little painful, so he said he had a ritual each night in which he would peel the adhesive back a millimeter at a time, and with each pull, he would plant a tiny, comforting kiss on Lucie's tender, pink skin. Imre eventually got rid of the flesh-colored patch altogether, replacing it with a nice black pirate one secured with an elastic band – obviously a superior solution.

You'll notice I've toggled in these anecdotes between calling him Imre and Sébastien. It's just because I'd already gotten so accustomed to calling him by his musical moniker.

So. Despite his discretion, we were getting to know each other. And because he's discreet, I hesitate to tell you this. But I'm sure you're wondering, and of course I'll ask him if it's okay to say this. I think he'll say it's okay. One night, a few days into that first visit, we'd been talking like that on my couch, and I was leaning in to hear him – I told you, he's quite soft-spoken – and he paused, and looked at me with a slightly nervous, sideways glance, as though he wanted to say something else but wasn't sure if he should. And I thought I knew what it was, and I wanted badly to kiss him, so I swiveled over, sat in his lap, looked him straight in the eyes, and pressed my mouth against his.

For all that I've said he can seem, sometimes, transparent, in that moment Imre fully materialized.

It's funny, before he ever came to New York, he'd written a jaunty little duet for us called "Pizzicato, Moderato, Cantabile," which said: "Amour, okay, love, all right, but on the tips of your toes, very light…" There was some spry wordplay using musical terminology to recommend a light-hearted, delicate approach to love. In retrospect, it seems pretty obvious that Imre was talking to himself. His natural approach to matters of the heart and its expressive organs is, frankly, *con fuoco*. Of course, I didn't know that then, but when I was recording my vocal track on the song, I improvised a little spoken interjection: "Doucement!" Gently! Well, Imre's a very gentle man, but sometimes he doesn't know his own strength. I have to say "doucement" with some regularity. He's always very apologetic if he gets carried away.

Anyway, after I climbed onto his lap, we ended up in my room, and that's where I discovered his webbed toes, and a few other interesting surprises. All delightful.

That's also why, a few days after our gig, we decided, mutually and spontaneously, that he should extend his stay by a week or so. And after a few more nights of exploration on my bed, and a few more of those little storytelling sessions on my couch and on my balcony, he finally looked at me once again with that slightly nervous, side-ways glance, and asked me if I really wanted to hear that other story, the one about the origins of Imre Lodbrog.

Well. Who wouldn't?

Chapter 4
High School

IN THE 1960S, Paris was indeed a movable feast. To be fifteen years old in '67, what more could one desire? But to be shut up in some single-sex barracks on the Avenue de la République for seven years, well, that seriously limited the party. Voltaire High School was a prison. To escape it, we had two solutions: the Père-Lachaise Cemetary, and music. To skip class and explore the tombs, in the somber maze where the soul of Jim Morrison would come to keep company with those of Allan Kardec, Méliès and so many others, was a delectation in keeping with our readings of the day, Lautréamont among others.

On the other side, there was the great sunny door of music. In October, 1962, I'm ten years old, in the fifth grade, and The Beatles release "Love Me Do." The entire path of my life will be determined by that. A rampant identification with the Fab Four which will continue throughout their discography. The year in which I leave high school, The Beatles separate. In between, the world has changed. It's gone from black and white to color. From silent to singing. We've passed through Flower Power, a myriad of groups and singers have flourished, some magicians as well as musicians. We Voltairians have been lifted up and carried by these flows and currents along with youth all over the planet.

The multiple horizons of our lives have conjoined in one great dream.

Frédérique Tchékovitch, AKA Freddy, wore pink outfits and high-heeled boots, on account of a slight complex about his height. He wasn't particularly short, he just wished he were bigger. He was a very goodlooking kid, and he wore pomade in his hair, parted in the middle, falling in waves on either side of his somewhat feminine face, sort of like France Gall in that period. Seeing him, you had the impression of a dandy. But a slightly sickly dandy, a little cross and choleric, oversensitive, as if he felt something were rubbing against his inner nature. He'd get bothered by the slightest thing. Most often because of wounded vanity.

All that, I'd heard about second-hand. Because Frédérique Tchékovich and I were anything but pals. He didn't even want to hear my name, he avoided me in the hallways at school and walked out of any party where I showed up. I never knew why, not then, not later. I suppose it was some sense of rivalry.

In those vast barracks of Voltaire High School, populated by about two thousand pre-adolescents and adolescents exclusively of the masculine sex (they dangled the hope of integrating with a girls' school up to my last moment there, though it didn't happen), we two were the most visible elements. Him, with his lacquered hair and his pink outfits, me with my shoulder-length mop of frizz and my harlequin suits: orange shirt, baker's pants, mauve jacket and green Clarks. Freddy and I, we really noticed one another. To tell the truth, there was also a certain Charlie, his raggy mane styled after the band Cream, who claimed to be Johnny Hallyday's nephew. But he wasn't a musician. Whereas Tchékovitch and I... Well, at least Tchékovitch was.

Me, I scratched out some chords. From the age of five to that of fifteen, compelled by my parents, I'd taken piano lessons. But as with most kids, it quickly became an obligation rather than a pleasure. After ten years of good and loyal service, just when I'd gotten to the level of Beethoven's *Piano Sonata No. 14*, I abdicated. Naturally, I'd come to regret this decision – and I still regret it. In fact, when I find myself in a room with a piano in it, I stand off to the side, awkwardly, like one does with an ex that one's dropped. Unless the room is empty, in which case, I timidly approach it and plunk out a few chords, reviving my regrets. Since then, I've held a morbid and quasi-masochistic passion for piano music, which is deeply tied to my childhood. And when I really want to make myself suffer, I listen to Debussy, Liszt, or, worst of all, Chopin. I wrote a song with the title, "Chopin is an Assassin..."

But at the age of fifteen, I didn't actually give up on music. I just passed from the keyboard to the fretboard.

The guitar, as the epoch demanded, drew me like a magnet. Still, I'll never have the ambition of becoming a good guitarist in any particular style. For that, I'd have to work, and on the guitar, all I'm seeking is pleasure – as in the rest of my life. My first guitar was a classical one, nylon strings, a good thick fretboard for working on bar chords. Quickly, I started to hum little melodies, and images came to me that transform into words that stick to the little tunes I hum. At sixteen, I birthed my first song: *"Les pieds dans l'eau."*

Freddy, for his part, had already attained the stature of a Guitar Hero. I had the chance to hear him once or twice (at Richard Kolinka's house for example), and that was enough to instill boundless admiration for that disagreeable little guy. It appeared to be a gift from the heavens, such rock 'n' roll mastery and virtuosity at the age of fifteen, sixteen! It was astonishing. But the key to the mystery was in the work it took. Him, he hadn't been sentenced to the piano by his parents, but to the accordion. At that time, the accordion was the symbol of good old French popular music – the exact opposite of rock 'n' roll. For him, the guitar was an act of retaliation, almost of revenge.

Tchékovitch was as hard on his fretboard as he was on the rest of the world. Days and nights spent working on riffs, ascents, descents, phrasing, faithfully reproducing the music we all heard spinning on our 45s. His masters were the masters of the moment: Hendrix, Clapton, Richards, Townsend, Page… Through hard work and talent, he'd integrated in record time, note for note, that whole fabulous repertoire.

At Voltaire in those years, there were more or less

three rock groups per class. We all wallowed in the myth of our cult groups – The Beatles, The Stones, The Who, The Kinks. We thought we were them, we grew our hair long and we practiced. Since none of us knew much about what we were doing, with the exception of Tchékovitch, we distributed our roles somewhat arbitrarily. You, you look like Ringo, so you'll be the drummer. Your pout is bigger than Jagger's, you can be the singer, me, I have a guitar, him, he's got his parents' piano… We spent hours drooling at the window of the Paul Beuscher Music Store, spending our last dimes on cheap knock-offs. Our drum sets were usually composed of detergent boxes and pots and pans. So as not to despair in our obscurity, we pinned our hopes to some possible wedding or bar mitzvah where we might have our first concert.

The music that came out of all that wasn't worth much – a few slightly mangled covers, a couple of lame originals. But the important thing was having an attitude and the right clothes, hooked as we were on pop music and its iconography. To nourish our passion for rock, there were concerts at The Olympia and its enormous musicoramas. I saw, among others, The Animals, The Troggs, The Beach Boys, The Who, Donovan, and an unforgettable concert by The Flock with their crazy violinist, which went from the afternoon till after midnight. Better still, under The Olympia there was a sort of cave where the concerts took on a nearly cabaret style. I saw The Moody Blues there and each member gave me an autograph. I sat at the bar and discussed the show with Cat Stevens, who lent me his guitar and let me pick out a chord or two.

And then, one morning in 1968, it was the month of May. May '68. A month that will remain, for better or worse, always tied to the idea of revolution. For better, because things did change after that. For worse, because in fact, nothing really changed. France still drags along its molted shell. But the maxims "It's forbidden to forbid!," "Be realistic and demand the impossible!," these were still beautiful to see scrawled across the walls of Paris. There was also "Art is shit!" – as for that, no comment.

I was sixteen years old, my political conscience was what it would remain: nebulous and utopian, though in great part repulsed. No presidential candidate has ever motivated me enough to cross the street and put a ballot in the urn. I say that with neither pride nor shame. I've only voted once in my life, the first time Le Pen emerged as a serious risk. I hate the laziness that confuses right and left, but both sides played a part in the rise of Le Pen. I hear the same howling wolves. I vaguely recall a speech by Mitterrand in '81 that moved me, because for the first time, I had the sense that there was something human in the message. But even if it was sincere, on the day of the elections, I was in Sri Lanka.

So, May '68, for me like for many others – well, it was a big party. The locks were blown open. We could skip class and take the subway without paying. Unfortunately, for many students, that presented certain tempations, some of which took a nasty turn. A few of our teachers had been pretty rough in the past, using old-school teaching methods and non-stop punishment, but the price they paid for that seemed to me inhuman, I won't dwell on the details. But, to give you an idea,

Mme. Bleu, a sexagenarian physics teacher, ended up pinned to the ground under a shower of pissing students. Another committed suicide, leaving a note in his office: "My students killed me." A father who came to to pick up his kid found himself beaten up by a gang led by his own son.

It was a free-for-all. Protests everywhere you turned. I went to a few, joining the throngs in the Latin Quarter and getting stoned on the tear gas wafting through the streets. But I never threw a stone, and I found the slogan "CRS/SS" – equating the national guard with the Nazi paramilitary forces – a brutal exaggeration. To tell the truth, I often pitied them, the CRS guards, who were about the same age as the students. Stewing for hours in their military outfits, awaiting orders while spit and insults rained down on them… So not surprisingly, when the orders came, their reaction was rabid.

The Latin Quarter was a powder keg, a volcano, and it was all of France that was ready to blow. Aragon and Sartre predicted a brighter future, leading the masses out of the factories and into the streets, swirling the workers into the spiral. The student leader Cohn-Bendit, "Dany the Red," seemed to be on every corner. De Gaulle described the chaos as "shitting in your own bed" ("*La réforme oui, la chie-en-lit non!*"), then found himself in the bullseye zone. But they didn't understand the man, who quickly called in the army. Columns of tanks rolled into Paris, at least that's what they say.

And then there was the referendum, the plebiscite, the counter-protests on the Champs-Elysées. De Gaulle stayed in power and order was restored, in a manner of speaking. They took care of the most urgent sites first, the universities and the factories. The high schools remained in a state of total chaos, virtually without administrative oversight. You could go to class or not, punch a teacher in the face, set fire to the classrooms. The headmaster stayed holed up in his office, afraid of being taken hostage, which in fact happened a few times.

As for Voltaire High School, the only possible solution was to let the national guard surround the place. They were quickly met with a hailstorm of tables and chairs thrown through windows. Some real battles took place, at all hours, but I spent the next few months largely at two nearby bars, the Cristal and the Fontenoy, putting change in the jukebox, smoking Gauloises and trying to flirt with the girls from Hélène Boucher, the closest all-girls school. The neighboring cafés were our neutral territory. That's where my friend Olivier met Catherine, with whom he'd end up spending the rest of his life.

Roland Barthes came to dinner at my parents' house that summer. When the question was posed to him: "So, May '68, revolution or not?," he contented himself with a smile as slender as the new moon.

As far as I was concerned, the bigger revolution was happening in music. The double *White Album* had just come out, and it was in every record store – still in the wake of *Sgt. Pepper's*, a musical Ali Baba's cave. From "Martha My Dear" to "Helter Skelter," without a doubt the most fabulous pop/rock voyages ever pressed onto vinyl. Olivier and I listened to it over and over on the high-fi turntable at his sister's apartment. We had no idea how deeply we were being branded by the hot iron of what we were listening to.

The music of the era awakened our creativity—but it also condemned us forever. He and I, like millions of others across the globe, shut ourselves up in an impossible bubble with devastating, incurable effects. How many jokers have I known, and do I still know, who were infected with a sickness that would eat up their lives, after dazzling them at first? We had no choice but to grab a guitar, to cling to music—with so little hope of achieving anything with it. A few became bankers, some emergency room physicians, but music remains the center of their universe, the axis of their orbit, and without it they'd surely fall fast and hard.

1968 brought one more revolution for me, my first acid trip. They say it's impossible to describe color to a blind person. So I won't even try to tell what happened to me in Scotland. Beyond dreams and pseudo-reality, I simply discovered a different dimension. That was the epoch of "Yellow Sunshine," "Purple Haze," and a few other space capsules that projected you into an unknown universe with all five senses on overload. No way to direct it, you just had to hold on and enjoy it. Hearing colors, seeing sound waves, chasing after your own thoughts, sudden and piercing, the great mysteries revealed themselves with a frenetic clarity. With the music and the protests, it all became part of my adolescent world view, as if it were all normal.

I refused to come down from that high for as long as possible. Later, in stages, I heard the era echoed in the rage of punk and in Pink Floyd's *The Wall*. Disco enacted a fatal burial. "The death of music," according to Freddy.

In '69, I switched from six to twelve strings, and

there, I really began to find pleasure, mixed with the pain of strings that cut into my fingers until they bled. My father, who was working at an advertising agency, had a big client in New Caledonia. The guy heard my songs and loved them. He proposed a project that I never really understood, but which took me into a recording studio for the first time to record a .45 with four tracks, among them "Rendez-vous à Nouméa." Words by Robert Régnier, music by his son. I never really found out what happened to that record.

At the end of '69 into '70, I stopped by my high school now and then, but mostly I lived among the communes, with free love, LSD, 'shrooms, Tantric delirium and psychedelic music. With my twelve strings, I took on the role of troubadour and spun out jams for the motley crowds. My guitar became my secret weapon. One beautiful, starry night on a full acid trip in the Normandy countryside, sitting in a field, I attracted a herd of cows who made a circle around me. That's where I met my first true love. Christine, a pseudo-student at the Bourges Art School, but true hippie, living in a floating bubble between the Brothers Grimm and Krishna.

I was at the end of my studies, but I'd definitely left school behind, quitting Voltaire just a few months before the Baccalauréat and refusing to listen to my parents' appeals to reason. I took my guitar in one hand, Christine by the other, and headed to Marrakesh! After bumming around smoking kif in the Medina, I parachuted into the Victor Hugo School of Marrakesh just long enough to pick up my Bac, pulling it out of my ass.

When I returned to France, my crew from Voltaire had dispersed. Only one friend remained, Olivier Cauquil and over the next few decades, I saw him regularly. At the time, I was sure Freddy and I would never see each other again. Aside from his nasty character, his pink outfits and his phenomenal chops on the guitar, he was now practicing hypnosis and claiming to be a spiritual medium. I never had the chance to verify it, although I once challenged him: "Oh yeah? Fine. Just try to hypnotize me!"

Chapter 5
The Eastern European Tour

AFTER IMRE'S FIRST VISIT, it became clear that our collaboration would continue. I had those ideas about an international tour, but first I invited him back to New York. I wanted to hear more of his stories.

As you now know, Freddy had identified Sébastien early on as his high school rock 'n' roll rival. Imre insists that back then he was just a shy, awkward kid, strumming a few half-assed chord progressions and croaking on top, while Freddy practiced like a madman, nailing every classic recorded solo of the period. Imre claims to have no idea why Freddy was threatened by him, but in fact, each of them would have his proverbial fifteen minutes of fame, or at least get tantalizingly close to it: Freddy was briefly the guitarist with a band that blew up, eventually opening for The Rolling Stones in Paris. But by that time, Freddy, a major hot-head, had already stormed out of a practice session and been replaced. As for Sébastien, a few years later he was discovered by a producer who conscripted him as one of the "new hopes of French song" – a TV project that morphed, briefly, into a touring group. A couple of the other "new hopes" went on to have very high-profile careers, particularly Hervé Cristiani, who would become a French pop icon in the '80s, and Imre's close friend for life. In fact, it was Cristiani, not Iggy Pop, that Imre had been referring to when he said he'd shown my ukulele cover to a musical buddy of some renown. Unfortunately, it didn't look like Imre was going to smash the charts like Hervé anytime soon. His shyness and sensitivity necessitated a certain amount of self-medication in order for him to get up on stage (hello, Jim Beam). There were a few other problems that might reductively be categorized as various forms of self-sabotage – but for now, suffice it to say that in the decade following high school, neither Freddy's nor Sébastien's star had risen quite as far as some people might have hoped.

I found this melancholy saga of near-misses very compelling. For his part, Imre seemed equally intrigued by my world. He willingly, if somewhat shyly, went along on all kinds of social and cultural outings I proposed. He seemed to like my eccentric friends, who also took immediately to him. From somebody else's perspective, I suppose the question would be: who was taking whom for a ride? Was he, as somebody had once suggested, an "old fox" who'd buffaloed me into creating a fantasy of a French rock star? Or was I a loopy postmodern novelist bent on incorporating him into my quirky life-as-art narrative? Somehow the answer to those questions didn't bother either of us. If somebody was taking somebody for a ride, it seemed to be mutual. Another way to say this is: Imre and I had become fellow travelers.

Perhaps I should tell you where I was when Imre was sporting colorful bell-bottoms at the Lycée Voltaire. Far, far away. In 1969, I was a mild-mannered seven-year-old in Madison, Wisconsin, just beginning my cello lessons under a graduate student at the UW. When she got too busy to teach me, she passed me off to her twin sister, also a cellist. I don't remember noticing the difference.

I knew virtually nothing of rock 'n' roll. I was an okay cellist, but mostly I was bookish. I listened to jazz and classical music, but in college I basically abandoned any musical aspirations for literary ones. I wrote poems and read a lot of French literature and I began to accrue a group of friends who would dress up in weird outfits and stage "happenings" and make unusual short films.

These people also knew virtually nothing of rock 'n' roll. My friends and I were also a little experimental in our approach to life, and sex. It went without saying, although we also said it, that we were feminists.

It was some years before I'd begin writing novels. They were, as I tried to explain to Imre, more influenced by French authors than by Americans. My attachment to Montaigne and Proust might explain something about my diaristic and memorialist tendencies. Then there's the question of my shamelessness, which, truth be told, has given my mother a bit of unease over the years. Vaginal Davis once compared me to "the young Françoise

Sagan," though the more obvious bad influences were probably Colette and Anaïs Nin.

I described Imre above as being "discreet," and indeed, on the topic of sexual relations, he's certainly more withholding than I am. But in relation to *affective* relations – well, that's where he's not afraid to let it all hang out. In fact, although it seemed clear early on that our affection was mutual, and very evenly matched, his unrestrained expressions of enthusiasm sometimes left me feeling a little awkward. Also, there was that Don Quixote thing of his, and I quickly discerned that, if you were to accept this literary comparison, I'd taken up the position of Dulcinea. This hasn't exactly diminished over time. At first, I thought maybe it was a problem with his eyesight, but in fact, his remains quite sharp. He only needs mild correction for reading. Still, he can get fairly moon-eyed when examining even features of mine that your average observer would probably categorize as flaws. Once he reached under my chin and dandled my small, incipient wattle. For a second I thought I was going to bean him, until I realized that he was looking at it as if it were the quintessence of pulchritude. He whispered, *"J'aime ça!"* I love that! I think we can pretty safely attribute that to romanticism.

Imre is not afraid to wear his heart on his sleeve. That's an interesting figure of speech. It seems to me very apt – the thought of exposing your inner organs on the outside of your clothing. Which is, I suppose, how many people feel about making public your erotic exploits. But to me, the much more naked thing is to expose the heart. I once wrote an unrhymed sonnet about that. It was based on one of Barthes's *Fragments d'un discours amoureux,* "Obscene." My poem began with this little epigraph from Barthes: "Discredited by modern opinion, love's sentimentality must be assumed by the amorous subject as a powerful transgression which leaves him alone and exposed; by a reversal of values, then, it is this sentimentality which today constitutes love's obscenity." I then described, as I'm wont to do, some dirty tidbits from a love affair, but concluded, again citationally:

> The thing that was obscene, the dirty secret,
> was neither flesh nor fetish. It was love
> itself. Bataille describes the sentiment
> in all of its vulgarity — a massive
> throbbing organ. An embarrassment.

So, while I may be a bit more circumspect than Imre about romance, it's my sexual frankness that occasionally baffles him — though he's always been intrigued by self-possessed women. I told you about his love of Etty Hillesum. He likes to think about women's issues in a broad historical and mythological context. Another of the first books he gave me was Michelet's *La Sorcière,* which is arguably a precursor to Silvia Federici's account of the development of autonomist feminism. I tend, as you can see, to articulate things in certain "isms," whereas Imre for years has tried to avoid those kinds of terms. He begrudgingly shrugs and nods now when I tell him he's an anarchist and a feminist. I guess I just wore him down.

Should I tell you how I brought him around? It was a bit of a *baptême du feu,* a combination of exposure to and participation in some of the art and life practices I thought would be good for him. He's been surprisingly game. One of the first stops was a queer-friendly Bikram yoga studio on the Lower East Side. Imre had had some sort of a yoga practice years ago in his hippie phase, but in recent years his relaxation, when he could get it, was largely accessed through chemical means. But he earnestly dripped sweat through the twenty-six postures, nearly every day on a special one-month pass I'd gotten him online. I also made him eat salad, drink water, and cut down from three lumps of sugar to two in his coffee.

I brought him along to performances by my friends and other artists I admired. We sat on pillows on the floor of a gallery while Carmelita Tropicana declaimed something with a jewel-encrusted breastplate on her boobs and feathers coming out of her head. There were psychedelic projections and the audience was snacking on dried figs. We went to see a very inventive piece by Narcissister which involved the retrieval of an astonishing number of the elements of her costume from a capsule enclosed in her vagina. (Imre was sincerely impressed by her dance technique – indeed, she's very graceful.) I took him to a concert by two of my students, a noise duo known as "Penis." He loved that.

But perhaps the outing he enjoyed most was The Feminist Ball at Joe's Pub – a fundraiser for the Feminist Press. He scratched his head when I invited him, and I imagine he was wondering if he might end up like Marcello Mastroianni in *City of Women*. That is, in over his head. But in fact, Justin Vivian Bond performed, and

Imre was utterly enchanted. Later, I read him a passage from Vivian's beautiful memoir, a passage about wearing V's mother's lipstick to school. The shade was Revlon's "Iced Watermelon." Imre said the specificity of that lipstick was like Proust's madeleine, and he ended up writing a song about it for Vivian. To write the song, he looked up the names of some other shades of Revlon lipstick. He liked the sound of "Fig Jam," so I bought some for myself. Imre likes lists of things. It was around this period that I also showed him the list of slang expressions for female masturbation that he would work into a little number called "Walking Fingers."

We made a few trips to the places Imre remembered from his previous visits to New York. He came for the first time in '72, at Rosie's invitation. A few months later, he joined her and Joelle for a cross-country trip that took a catastrophic turn on the way to Mexico. They were driving a gold Mercedes – the owner had hired them to get it south of the border, but some trucker in Kansas seemed to find it a provocation, three hippie kids in a rig like that, and he terrorized them, almost running them off the road. Then, on the way back from Mexico, the American border patrol didn't want to let Imre in with his French passport. The Mexicans didn't want him either. For eight days they had to hide out from both sides, and they spent two nights stuck in the middle of the Rio Bravo Bridge. Rosie had a raging fever. All their stuff got stolen. It was a nightmare.

He returned to New York a few times after that – recently enough to know that the city had changed. His last visit had been in 1998, when he was working on a short film by his friend Gregory. Still, he was pretty stupefied by Brooklyn's recent metamorphosis. The fancy bistros in Williamsburg baffled him. He insisted we spend an afternoon at Coney Island – that, at least, was still recognizable.

In addition to the sightseeing, I also managed to arrange some informal performances for us. While our bigger shows are quite carefully constructed and rehearsed, we're also happy to grab any opportunity to play out. If we get a drink ticket and can palm off a CD on an unsuspecting audience member or two, we feel it's been worth our effort. We played a few dive bars in Brooklyn over the din of clinking glasses and loud people talking on their cell phones. One was appropriately called the Trash Bar.

I also roped Imre into a multi-faith "food justice" gig at Judson Church, where we played a tune we'd composed about manna while a mother and son performed contact improvisation on the floor. Our act was followed by a group of very assertive Sikh sword fighters. The link between their act and "food justice" was not entirely clear. One of the performers took the microphone and politely but firmly told the audience that their performance had been mislabeled a "dance" in the program, while in fact they were executing a martial art. They then began piping what sounded like a very loud Bollywood soundtrack through the speakers and energetically clashed their weaponry.

All of this galavanting around the city was interesting, of course, but given our mutual migratory tendencies, both of us were developing an itch to take our show on the road. Why did we choose Eastern Europe for our first tour? Well, to tell the truth, it was a mix of arbitrary contacts, cheap tickets, dumb luck and, perhaps most worrisome of all, a certain naïve curiosity on my part. I don't mean curiosity about Imre – although it's true that half of his family roots lie in the region. I mean a naïve curiosity about a part of the planet that, at least in my childhood, had been represented to me as a kind of parallel universe, an upside-down world – something like the way Léry had imagined "Antarctic France." Of course, all that changed in 1989, when the wall came down, simultaneously unleashing a slew of personal liberties, as well as the violences of the unbridled "free" market economy.

1989 was also the year of Taylor Swift's birth, as indicated by the title of her extremely profitable album of that name – which sort of puts everything in a nutshell. You see, the global ascendency of neoliberalism has had all kinds of ramifications, and some of them are musical.   The popular music that surrounds us is so highly processed and homogenized, when you encounter somebody as unique and original as Imre, the obvious question that pops into your head is: "Why has nobody ever heard of this guy?" Another, slightly more romantic way of putting this is: "Where has Imre Lodbrog been all my life?" Of course there are a few plausible answers to this question, some of which may already be apparent to you, but I think it's also fair to say that in this story, one big, nefarious culprit in the invisibilizing of an artist of genius is the same one it so often is: capitalism.

When I unveiled this hypothesis to Imre, he didn't reject it outright – though he wasn't quite ready to jump on my communist curiosity bandwagon. I told you, he has an aversion to all isms – and his family history put him a little closer to some historical realities that I'd largely encountered in my childhood through the skewed lens of the cartoon *Bullwinkle*. But whatever misgivings he might have had about my grasp of history, he's always up for an adventure, and it doesn't take much prodding to get him to hit the road.

And so we hatched a plan for the Eastern European Tour. As I said, I'd mentioned to Imre I had a Latvian connection. I thought that might impress him, but he immediately countered with a contact in Lithuania. The Latvian connection was my old friend Kelly McKee, a hippie poet I met traveling in Brazil about thirty years ago. We'd remained in sporadic contact, and every once in a while he'd urge me to visit Riga, where he'd settled. He'd gone there on some sort of State Department junket as a roving official poet and decided to stay. There was later something of a national scandal involving his love life. He'd had an illicit affair with a beautiful young actress from the experimental theater scene named Muza, and she became pregnant with triplets. I can't say too much about it, but there were some political figures whose feathers were ruffled. Eventually the scandal died down, and Kelly now lives with Muza and the triplets.

He continues to write poetry. He sent me a link to a reading he did recently at a Riga bookstore. In the video, you can see Muza sitting behind Kelly in deep concentration as he reads from a collection of dirty ornithological limericks. There's another unidentified bookish figure sitting next to her who also appears to be taking the smutty bird poems very seriously, pensively rubbing his chin. I felt this boded well for our own reception in Latvia. When I wrote Kelly, he was very encouraging. He said he could probably get us a gig (for tips) at a club called "Taka," which was a "neat spot." He also said he might be able to hook us up in Olomouc, in the Czech Republic.

Regarding Imre's Lithuanian connection: perhaps it won't surprise you that she was of the female persuasion – an amateur lounge singer in Klaipéda with whom he'd been swapping complimentary messages online. The Lithuanian connection's name was Natalija Dombrovska. She'd started following me online as well. She said a couple of polite things about my vocal interpretations, so I responded warmly on a couple of hers. In fact, I think her voice is quite good. "Sultry" would be the aptest description. When I told her so, she said something about how it was nice to receive comments from *"une autre femme,"* as that happened relatively rarely. I said, *"Oui, c'est vrai, pourquoi ça?"* But Natalija didn't answer, and shortly after my first duet with Imre came out, her comments started to swing unpredictably from that sisterly solidarity to what sounded like outright hostility. I began to worry this might throw a wrench into our plans for the tour. I vaguely suspected Imre was hoping for a catfight. I thought it was time to do a little more research about her.

It didn't take long to realize I might have gotten myself into hot water. Dombrovska's YouTube videos were being uploaded by somebody named Boriss Gruba, surely her lover, and just a bit of Googling quickly revealed him to be a French national, and a high-level operative of the UMP with a history of involvement in the arms trade. He also had a sideline in cosmetic surgery. There was even photographic evidence of Dombrovska and Gruba schmoozing with the former French prime minister during a visit to Vilnius. In these photos, Dombrovska was identified as an associate of the "KLV Lithuania" – an entrepreneurial venture headed by Gruba, apparently aimed at advancing the neoliberal agenda throughout the former Soviet Bloc. A major component of the KLV's activities was "personnel information gathering" which I think we can all agree means "spying." I read all this with an increasing sense of dread, which climaxed when I noted the small print on the KLV's website disclosing that they were gathering information on the IP addresses of all visitors to their site.

I wrote Imre, "My goose is cooked." I told him about Dombrovska's lover Gruba and the arms trafficking. I asked Imre if he thought Gruba was aware of his existence. I told him to watch his back.

Imre purported to know nothing of this web of intrigue. In fact, he claimed not to know that Natalija Dombrovska had a lover at all. Still, periodically

Dombrovska would leave a comment on one of my tracks. I had the distinct impression that they were striking a competitive tone. One day I wrote Imre:

> bonjour imre. la lituanienne veut montrer son
> erudition. elle cite madame de sévigné sur mon
> cover of a very cheesy french pop song. is that
> because i cited colette on yours? elle me fait plus
> peur que ton passé criminel.

Hello Imre. The Lithuanian wants to show her erudition. She cites Madame de Sévigné on my cover… She scares me more than your criminal past… I'd posted a song about opinions, to which she had responded: *"Les opinions des femmes ne sont que la suite de leurs sentiments' – de Madame de Sévigné."* The opinions of women are merely the consquences of their sentiments. I chirpily answered that I shared her enthusiasm for the great epistolarian. I really can't make fun of her for trying to look high-brow. As my message to Imre indicated, I'd just been citing Colette on a track of his.

Let's face it: although our politics were wildly divergent, Natalija Dombrovska and I were flip sides of the same coin. But even Imre had to confess that his suspicions were aroused by a mystifying comment she left on one of his tracks, indicating that she had "the eye of the tornado and the ear of Moscow" to pronounce his artistic production *"superbe."* Imre gallantly responded, *"Je suis protégé alors!"* So I'm protected! But I'm sure he recognized the gamble in accepting Dombrovska's oversight.

I realize this sounds pretty unlikely, but I didn't make any of it up, although it's true that I've altered a few names and identifying factors, either out of discretion or self-preservation – maybe both.

But back to our story: My cheapo ticket on Air Baltic had a 24-hour layover at CDG – that's surely why it was so cheap, but it was lucky for me, because it meant I could meet Imre and we could hang out for a night in Paris before we flew to Riga the next afternoon. He mostly lives in a little shack in Normandy, but he grew up in Paris and his mother has a place there. He stays with her a couple of nights a week. He took me by to meet her.

Lili is utterly enchanting. She is, indeed, petite, and impressively spry for her age, which is ninety-six. She lives in the 11th arrondissement, on the rue de la Folie-Méricourt. When we arrived, Lili asked Imre to get us some Suze, a yellow French liqueur made from gentian root. He brought it on a tray with some small fancy glasses. We clinked them together and said, *"Narok,"* which is Romanian for "Cheers!" I was familiar with it because Imre says it all the time.

Lili received us in Imre's father's study, which she'd left exactly as it was when he passed away ten years ago. His writing desk was cluttered with strange little objects – rocks, bones, feathers, and small carvings. There was a preserved owl on the wall, and some surrealistic drawings he'd made, and a few photographs, including this one of Imre as a boy:

Lili and her son look so much alike – except that even as a boy his expression seemed to communicate some kind of internal struggle.

She put her hand on my arm and told me there was one other word I needed to learn, this one in Hungarian, and that I should pull it out any time Imre got overwrought. "Izgága." She said that if he got jumpy, the trick was to look him in the eye and say calmly, *"Ne sois pas izgága."* I wasn't sure how functional this was, but I practiced saying it a few times.

Perhaps you're wondering why the salad of Romanian and Hungarian. Lili's family hails from Cluj – the unofficial capital of Transylvania, which has had a complicated history. Imre told me that his mother's identity papers classified her ethnicity as "mosaïque." That wasn't actually about the salad of Romania and Hungary. It was a reference to the people of Moses.

It was Imre's father who hid her (along with her mother) during the war. Each of Imre's parents' stories deserves its own novel, but I'll give you the bare bones of both. Lili's father, Imre Szekely, died when she was just two. She often says that the absence of her father, who was by all accounts a stand-up guy, was a lack she felt all her life. Her mother, Mathilde, was sweet-natured, but a little disconnected from the practical realm. She'd lost not only her husband, but also two children to illness. Though Imre Szekely had been a rather wealthy banker, Mathilde was swindled by his colleagues out of his fortune after his death, so Lili's childhood was one of extreme poverty. Her older sister, Bözsi, went to Bucharest to make her way, and Lili was left with their fragile mother to take in boarders. Lili was spirited and pretty, but she was often ostracized at school for being Jewish. She had to take on all kinds of small jobs to bring some money into their household. Her childhood passion for the French language and culture led her, later, to pursue university studies in French literature.

Robert Régnier, meanwhile, had just quit his post teaching in a parochial school in Paris. He was planning an adventure in Mexico.

He was in London preparing his departure when war broke out. It wouldn't have been difficult for him to get out of Europe before being mobilized, but he had a kind of fantasmatic revelation that if he didn't serve, some other young guy might end up getting a bullet intended for him. He joined the 123rd regiment, and was quickly captured. He was held in Stalag 17, in Austria, where he largely spent his time crafting letters home for his unlettered fellow prisoners. He requested, and was granted, a transfer to a work farm in Slovenia where they were farming beets. He escaped briefly with another guy, but was caught and shipped back to Stalag 17, and then Rava-Ruska, a camp on the border of Poland. Then he got sent to Vienna, to an arms factory. He refused that work, citing the Geneva Conventions, and eventually got transported to Hennersdorf, where he spent a year making bricks instead – and imagining his next escape. He had a couple of little amorous adventures with some Czech girls who were also working at the brick factory.

It was October of '42 when he managed yet another breakout. His plan was to cross the Hungarian border and get to the French Embassy in Budapest, and then go on to Romania and then Turkey, where the French resistance was holding out. From there, he hoped to make his way to London to join De Gaulle's troops. But after a month of nocturnal fugitivity, arriving in Budapest, a diplomat gave him another suggestion – to take a teaching position in Kolozsvàr – the Hungarian name for Cluj, which was then a part of Hungary. Kolozsvàr was on the way to Turkey, so Robert accepted the post. That was in January of '43. It was snowy, and there was Gypsy music playing everywhere, which stirred something in him, despite his generally reserved disposition.

He actually loved the teaching gig as well, and it was at the university that he met Lili, an ambitious and charming graduate student who asked him to read her thesis on Henri Monnier, the French playwright and caricaturist. He somewhat impulsively told her that he'd love to read it, but that it might take him a whole lifetime. She also somewhat impulsively said that that might be possible, but that she and her mother were a package deal.

He got to know Lili's extended family. They traveled by bicycle to visit her cousins in Nagyvarod. They would, like much of Lili's family, eventually be gassed in the camps.

Starting in '42, the Germans occupied Kolozsvàr and the Jewish community was gradually "invited" to stay at some "alternative" camps – which were, in fact, antechambers to Auschwitz and Dachau. Some of Robert's Jewish students were considering going, thinking this might be a temporary and livable situation until things settled – but Robert had witnessed firsthand what was going on. He's seen the smoke rising from the gas chambers. By March of '44, his main pedagogical mission was helping his students figure out how to get the hell out of town on anything besides the horrific cattle cars. He hid Lili and her mother in the French Cultural Center, and quickly married Lili so she could get French papers. In order to marry Robert, Lili was forced, by law, to convert to Catholicism. There were a lot of close calls. Even when the Russians liberated the city, it wasn't the immediate relief they'd hoped for: the Russians suspected Robert of being a *Pétainiste*, and he was detained. Lili miraculously managed to negotiate his liberation with Vychinsky and Vinogradov themselves. Finally they made it to Bucharest, where they ended up staying and teaching until '48.

That time in Bucharest was evidently pretty interesting. That's where they befriended Jean Sirinelli, Roland Barthes, and Jean Rebeyrol. From there they moved to Egypt for another teaching gig. They left Cairo in 1952, and Lili was pregnant with Sébastien. He was born in Paris, but was conceived, according to Lili, in the Red Sea. In the water. Lili was thirty-two when she had her son. It was a difficult birth. She said his head was purple like an eggplant because they had to use forceps. (Years later, under psychoanalysis, Imre would wonder whether his birth-by-forceps had anything to do with the dread and panic he feels nearly every morning as he's first waking up.)

Lili's mother, Mathilde, continued to live with them, and she was a central figure in Imre's childhood. She never learned French. She and Imre developed a special pidgin language between the two of them, a mix of

Hungarian and French.

There's a lot more to tell but I'll stop here. I called this the "bare bones" of the story, and it is, though you may wonder how I know this much. Imre showed me some transcripts of interviews he did with his parents when they were already quite old. When he told Lili I'd read them, she asked him, wide-eyed, "You mean Barbara knows about my cousins in Nagyvarod? About Bözsi? She knows about the time Robert was almost sent to Siberia? She knows you were conceived in the Red Sea?"

He said, "Yes, she knows."

On the day that I met Lili, toward the end of our visit, Fatima arrived. She's a warm, attractive woman who appeared to be in her late thirties, though Imre later told me she was closer to my own age. Fatima is her devoted friend, and they have the complicity of schoolgirls. When Imre's not in town, Fatima spends the night at Lili's, and she's the one that makes it possible for him to travel sometimes.

Fatima embraced me and then sat close to Lili on the couch. She told me I looked just like my photograph.

She explained without an ounce of self-consciousness that after Imre had recorded a song with my name in it, she'd done a Google Images search and shown my picture to Lili. They both smiled.

Did I mention that Imre claims never to have Googled me?

The day after that meeting, Imre and I hit the road. On the way to the airport, we sang to each other, *sotto voce*, our road song, "Shuffle": It's a beautiful adventure, it's a beautiful car that zooms along on its own… As a going-away present, Imre's older daughter, Lucie, had given him a t-shirt with a picture of Keith Richards on it. He wore it on the plane to Riga. It looked great on him, because he and Keith Richards have that same craggy, wizened appeal. I took Imre's photo in his window seat so he could send it to Lucie.

When I look at the picture now, it's like a mise-en-abyme. I imagine Keith Richards just below where his image is cut off, with a picture of Imre on his t-shirt, with a picture of Keith on his t-shirt, with a picture of Imre… You get the idea. But it sort of begs the question: do rock stars wear t-shirts with pictures of other rock stars on them? Would Keith Richards get on a tour airplane wearing an Imre Lodbrog t-shirt?

I should explain our itinerary. Kelly had given me the email of the owner of that club called Taka – his name was Yuris. And Dombrovska had told Imre about a spot in Vilnius with the promising name "Café de Paris." Weirdly, when I wrote them, both places agreed to take us in! Well, maybe it's not that surprising, as I'd indicated that we'd be more than satisfied with a free beer as payment. Still, scoring two for two seemed to us pretty good for our first tour. Klaipéda, we learned, was basically just an industrial shipping port, without any major musical venues. Apparently most of Dombrovska's gigs there were at "private functions." But we'd need to pass through there regardless, as it was the main bus terminal on the way to Liepaja, the storied "rock 'n' roll capital of Latvia." Obviously, we needed to check that out. I researched the bus schedules and the rates at various flea-bag hotels before coming up with the road plan I began calling the "Latvia-Lithuania Loop." We'd be spending a couple of nights in each town, with the exception of Klaipéda, where we figured we'd just decamp for one night, hopefully without incident. Well, that was my hope. Imre might have been thinking something else.

The first thing we noticed when we landed in Riga was the ubiquity of leopard-print clothing. I noticed it anyway. It struck me that many of the men looked like potatoes, while nearly all the women, of whatever age, were quite beautiful – and nearly all wearing some form of faux wildlife. When I mentioned this to Imre, he claimed neither to have noticed their good looks nor their gaminess, although once I'd mentioned it he'd keep nudging me when another wildcat sauntered by.

We were both a little flummoxed by the cosmopolitanism of the city. Notwithstanding the leopard-print, a lot of people looked pretty stylish. The streets were charming, with lots of outdoor cafés and small, tasteful specialty shops. We found a restaurant with casually mismatched cups and saucers, chairs and banquettes, where we had some delicious fresh herring with an excellent white wine that was recommended by the waitress. After the meal, she brought us two perfect little cherry tarts, compliments of the chef. It was one pleasant surprise after another, and Imre and I couldn't help enjoying ourselves, even though this was hardly the adventure we thought we'd set ourselves up for. I mentioned that I, in particular, had some kind of suspect curiosity about a former-Soviet-bloc experience.

Oh well. We bashed on. We had a gig to do.

It turned out that Kelly couldn't actually make it to our show at Taka, as his triplets had a stomach virus and he and his wife Muza were busy cleaning up the projectile vomit. But Yuris was really nice. He appeared to be pretty stoned. At the gig, I have to say, Imre fucking killed it. Well, in truth, our audience was, as Imre later put it, five drunk Latvian guys laughing at their own jokes. But I think their enthusiasm was genuine. When we said we'd be playing our hit single, "Naked Lady with a Ukulele," they went fairly bananas over the title.

Next stop: Vilnius. It was nearly as picturesque as Riga. The sidewalk tables outside the Café de Paris were populated by louche smokers happy to chat Imre up in their serviceable French. We managed to get through our set without any major catastrophes, though at one point, acquiescing to a request from Imre, I did make the aesthetic blunder of attempting an interpretive dance. People pretended not to notice.

We stole one of the publicity posters.

We were fairly hammered.

We'd left the next day entirely open so we could explore the city. We took a few goofy photos of Imre in front of official buildings and statues of local heros. We turned a corner and that's when we stumbled onto… the *Genocido aukų muziejus*, or Museum of Genocide Victims.

We looked at each other and decided to step in.

As you can perhaps imagine, this was not exactly a cheerful experience. The building that houses the museum was constructed as the Court of the Vilnius Province of the Russian Empire. During the Nazi occupation, it was taken over by the Gestapo, and the walls of cell no. 3 in the basement still bear the inscriptions of Jewish prisoners who were later sent to the camps. After the war, the KGB moved in and began using those basement cells for interrogations.

Anybody who's thought much about atrocity tourism will tell you there's no way to do it right. I mean museologically, but of course there's really no way to take it in as an outsider to what went on in that building.

Imre and I stared at the photos of the Nazi resisters on the walls, many of them women. Imre was very quiet. I knew he was thinking about Lili, who lost so many people in the camps. But, in fact, this museum was mostly dedicated to subsequent atrocities: those of the KGB. Despite the schism in between, it seemed to present one seamless narrative of torture and murder. One can question the framing of the relationship between those two historical moments, but whatever one's political perspective, it was kind of hard not to be stupefied by the rapidity with which those basement cells had been repurposed. We sat on a bench outside afterwards and Imre cried a little, silently. We were pretty disoriented.

We bought ourselves a couple of beers in a convenience store and drank them quietly by the river. That's when we noticed the little footbridge leading to Užupis. The signage explained that the little district, which had been a Jewish neighborhood in the 16th century, had declared itself an independent republic in 1997. I'm not sure exactly how they got away with that. Apparently now it's occupied mostly by weirdos and expats. Around twilight, we crossed the footbridge into the hippie republic, and found a big marble wall engraved with a text in several languages: the Constitution of the Republic of Užupis. We stood and read it. There were 38 statements of basic rights, among them:

> Everyone has the right to be undistinguished and unknown.
> Everyone has the right to love and take care of the cat.
> Everyone has the right to look after the dog until

one of them dies.

A dog has the right to be a dog.

Everyone has the right to appreciate their unimportance.

Everyone has the right to understand.

Everyone has the right to understand nothing.

Everyone has the right to be misunderstood.

That helped.

The next day we headed to Klaipéda, which, as predicted, was on the industrial side, but not quite as grim as we'd expected. The name of the city, apparently, means "flat foot," and there was a weird stone monument with an enormous footprint in it. Of course I couldn't look at that without thinking of Boriss Gruba. Imre laughed at my paranoia, but while we were sitting having a meal at an outdoor café, I got a terrifying anonymous text trying to warn me about some character using the code name "Kropotkin."

You surely think I'm making that up, but it's surprisingly close to the truth. Anyway, it led to a brief snit between myself and Imre – I guess what you'd call our first fight. He'd been waffling over whether he'd contact Dombrovska. We'd been intentionally vague about our plans because I had a very uneasy feeling about her and Gruba. I felt this Kropotkin business just confirmed my suspicions. Imre thought I was being ridiculous.

We got in an argument in which I stormed off, and he ghosted me for a while and then got pissed off in turn, so he stormed away in the other direction, and we just barely managed to keep each other on our respective radars while acting like a couple of adolescents, when Imre himself received a message that put our childishness in perspective.

It was a text from Martine, the wife of Imre's friend Hervé Cristiani.

She said, "The battle's over."

Imre knew what she meant, though he didn't want to believe it. Hervé had been diagnosed with advanced lung cancer some time ago, and had been following a naturalist and macrobiotic regimen after allopathic therapies had proven useless. All healing practices require, of course, some leap of faith, and Imre had wanted to lend his to Hervé's hopes for a cure. For my part, I certainly didn't want to dampen Imre's. But I think Martine's message wasn't completely unexpected for either of us.

Imre told me that after his first visit for the show at the Hôtel Particulier, he had written Hervé and told him about me, and Hervé had said, "Oh, I really have to get better so I can meet this Browning character!" When Imre had first mentioned to me the name of his old friend, I'd Googled him, and listened to his music, and looked at some photographs. Really, he was very touching. When he was young, he looked like an angel.

Hervé had always been on Imre's case about his music. I explained that they met through their mutual designation as two of those "new hopes" for French song, and even though Hervé was the one who'd had the smash hit, he never lost admiration for Imre's songwriting skills. He'd gotten a little exasperated, over the years, with Imre's apparently inexhaustible capacity to undermine his own potential.

When Hervé became ill, it was bad enough that Imre was facing the possibility of losing his dear friend. But there was another ominous thing about the nature of the illness: Hervé and Imre had spent years puffing up parallel smokestorms – largely weed. Needless to say, Imre began to ponder the condition of his own lungs. Well. The message from Martine hit him hard. Imre's lost so many people, many much too early. No matter how prepared he might have been for this one, it was a blow. So naturally our trivial tiff evaporated. We spent our last hours in Klaipéda with his head on my shoulder, thinking about his friend.

The next day we departed for Liepaja, and I tried to distract Imre with the sights. The city was every bit as weird and great as advertised. There was rock 'n' roll memorabilia everywhere you turned. All the young people were attractively pierced and tattooed. They gave the hipsters of Williamsburg a run for their money. Strangely, though, we couldn't find any live music at all. Still, we stayed in a very stylish and cheap hotel run by some Danish electric guitarist called Louis Fontaine. There were some dimly lit chambers in this hotel with ornate, gold-leafed furniture.

Oddly, we never seemed to run into any other guests. We'd practice on the damask sofas under the smoky light of the tasseled floor lamps. The hotel was also a short walk to the beach, where I did yoga on the sand while Imre gamboled in the surf.

We really loved it there. Imre slowly absorbed the blow of Hervé's passing in the midst of that mix of rock 'n' roll attitude and uncanny quietude. We were sad to leave, but we told ourselves we'd be back one day.

Chapter 6
The Dead End

AFTER HIGH SCHOOL, I had no desire whatsoever to shut myself up in a university. The world was too vast and too tempting, and anyway, my obsessive notion of time told me there wasn't enough of it to spare.

I had a strange and binding attraction to the desert, to burning and unlimited horizons. Breaking all ties, I hit the road, hitchhiking from Porte d'Orlean all the way to the south of Senegal, passing through Morrocco, the Canary Islands, the former Spanish Sahara, and Mauritania. Four months roaming through Africa, marked by special encounters, among them two uncommon American girls: Rosie and Joelle. Our first meeting was in Las Palmas, the second was in Dakar, where we exchange addresses before saying goodbye. The next day, Christmas day, they took a plane to Paris. I gave them my parents' phone number so they could say hello from me. In fact, they'd all ended up celebrating New Year's Eve together.

Finally, out of money, somewhat discouraged, I went back to Paris myself. There, a letter from Rosie was waiting for me. How could I forget that envelope? It was pierced with a little hole on top, on the right, with a bit of string tied there, and inside the simple words: "The other end of the string is tied to my doorknob."

A beautiful and timely invitation to New York. But

in order to get there, I needed to get back on my feet, financially. By hook or by crook, I got myself the most incredible job: as a tour guide in Paris for groups of foreigners invited there by the Minister of Education. Me, who had dreamed of spitting rock lyrics into a microphone, suddenly found myself using one to reel off historical commentaries on a bus stuffed with tourists. I set myself to work learning about the city, but I confess that in the beginning, just to fill my spiel, I was pretty good at improvising some interesting "facts." "It was on the second floor or this building that Victor Hugo encountered Juliette Drouet…" A few other inventions would earn me compliments like, "This is our fifth time in Paris, but we learned a lot of things with you that we'd never heard before – thank you so much."

On 4 July 1972, Independence Day in the United States, I flew to New York, my pockets nicely lined. My plane landed at JFK around midnight. I was trembling with excitement and nervousness. New York in '72 wasn't what it is today. That was the time of *Taxi Driver*, of *The Panic in Needle Park*, of 42nd Street rotten with sex business, haunted with pimps, prostitutes and drag queens. James Brown was headlining at the Apollo. The Bowery looked like the Court of Miracles. As for Brooklyn, where I ended up for a few months with Rosie, I felt like I'd landed back in Dakar. The heat was stifling, the vegetation was astonishing, and the population was 98% black, many of the women dressed in colorful boubous. Except that instead of hearing the kora, I was bathed in the voices of Bessie Smith and Billie Holiday.

Of course I'd brought my guitar with me. Joelle introduced me to her friend Matthew, a skilled composer and flautist. He proposed that we do some busking in the streets. We practiced a few pieces each day, a mix of my tunes and folkloric airs from all over the world, and soon there we were, out on 5th Avenue, with my guitar case opened like a clam, and a cardboard sign saying, "Trying to get back to Paris." I quickly had to add, "Paris, France," since more than one passerby asked if we're from Paris, Ontario.

Large groups gathered around us. The quarters rained into my case. So did dollars, and fivers, and even tens, and even, believe it or not, once... Matthew, still blowing into his flute, elbowed me in the ribs, indicating a scrawny silhouette who stepped out of the circle and dropped a twenty into the case: Miles Davis himself.

A hundred meters away, an old Visigoth was squatting on the sidewalk selling the scores of his own compositions. The Visigoth was called Moondog.

Now and then, somebody would slip me a joint or a nice word or two with a telephone number. Sometimes large crowds pressed in around us. Our little business turned out to be pretty profitable. I attributed this to Matthew's skill on his enchanted flute.

One day, I saw a poster on the street and I couldn't believe my eyes: a concert by John Lennon in Madison Square Garden. One of my great regrets is never seeing The Beatles on stage. They came through Paris twice, in '64 and '65, but I was too young to go, or so I thought, imagining I'd have plenty of time later on. Back then it seemed like the Fab Four would be unending. Who would ever believe they'd pass like a comet?

Over the years, I got to see McCartney about fifteen times. But Lennon! That was something not to miss. He'd just moved to New York and that was the only concert he'd ever give there. To my great surprise, my friends didn't deign to buy a ticket. So I had that experience all to myself. Sha Na Na and Stevie Wonder opened for him, and then it was Lennon with his backing band, Elephant's Memory... Plus Yoko, with her primal screams.

But New York was just the first stop for Matthew and me. We were soon rich enough to head out on a "tour" of Canada, which both of us wanted to visit. After our first night in Montreal, after a few hours in the streets, I could barely pick up my case full of change— enough to pay for a king's feast. From there, we headed to Toronto and by chance, stumbled onto a festival. One of the organizers gave us a full day on the main street. Toronto, with its bars and gogo clubs was a true Byzantiaum!

Matthew was also a composer, immersed to his neck and gifted with perfect pitch. Everywhere he went, he scribbled notes on scraps of paper and woke up every morning gesticulating symphonies. But with my meager knowledge of music theory, his scores didn't look like anything I'd seen before. They looked like Japanese calligraphy, with notes mostly outside the musical staff. Matthew was into serial music, so it was pointless to look for the melody and harmony. Everything clashed, went against the grain, and was algebraic to my profane ears. Schöenberg, Alban Berg, Boulez, Berio, Webern were his masters.

His technical knowledge of music impressed me. I

suddenly felt illiterate, like somebody who can't read the language he speaks. I asked him to initiate me. He gave me a few lessons, and finally, a few months later, when I went back to France with what I learned in New York, I passed, miraculously, the entrance exam to the Ecole Normale de Musique de Paris.

All of a sudden, at the age of twenty, I decided to quit traveling and get serious. Finally a path lay ahead of me, and not just any path. With true passion, I threw myself into music theory, harmonic analysis, the history of music.

The Ecole Normale de Musique was from another century. To enter it was to step back in time. The décor, the scent, the old varnished wood, the characters thriving there, it felt like a delicious and anachronistic place. They couldn't give a rat's ass for rock 'n' roll. There, I met a remarkable young girl, who also parachuted in from another era. Fine, delicate, transparent. A pianist. Marie-Isabelle. I was afraid I'd break her just by looking at her. She spent about eight hours a day in front of the piano, and you could hear it. Her Fauré's "Nocturne" moved me to tears.

Because of Marie-Isabelle, the piano still inspires an unbearable melancholy in me to this day. I didn't understand what happened with her. And most of all, I didn't understand what didn't happen. She lived with her parents, in Vincennes, overlooking the railway. A few years after I met her, she threw herself under a train.

Outside of school, my life was that of a thug. My room was on a little dead end that bore my name: Saint-Sébastien. I never really liked that saint. Too many arrows sticking out all over. That dead end was a kind of

95

fool's nave, the kind revisited by Marcel Carné, the old popular Paris, with its interloping fauna. Water, gas and adultery on every floor. Downstairs from my apartment, an unbelievable little bistro became my headquarters. Drinking binges, stupid tricks, a lot of drifting. Every day around noon, I emerged from the haze, asking myself what I did the night before, promising myself I'd stop drinking. My love life was incoherent, and invisible. My one true companion was my dog, Java. A cream and chestnut mutt, with whom I shared my bed, and who shared her dog food with me.

I was losing my hair at the speed of light. When I'd take a shower, I'd leave the tub covered in it. When the wind blew, tufts would fly off. And it was my beautiful youth that I saw blowing away with it.

The summer of '73, New York came to Paris with a visit from Rosie and Matthew. Matt and I had decided to try it the other way around. If we had worked so well on the other side of the Atlantic, why wouldn't we go over well here, too? We made a "tour" of France, then Scotland—but the Europeans hold their purse strings tighter than the Americans. We barely managed to pay for our daily hamburger.

One day, in the Chaussée d'Antin metro station, as we finished a little Yiddish folkloric tune, a guy approached us: "Do you know some others like that?" In the chit-chat that ensued, I bluffed, not even knowing why: "Jewish folkloric music, that's our specialty!" The guy turned out to be a producer, and he proposed that we record an album on Arion Records, at the time the premier global production house for traditional music. For six days, we ingested the classics of the genre, and I added a couple of tunes of my own composition. And for peanuts, we ended up recording the album, which would later come out on the Arion label, with Matthew credited as the flautist and me, strangely, appearing under the name of Lehakat Ha Nodedim... Apparently Greenbaum sounded more Jewish than Régnier.

On our return, I went back to school. That music school was, for me, the only structure I could hold onto, a sort of skeleton in my mushy life, a hope of redemption. I managed to get good grades on my exams, but I just couldn't hold on for the duration. The die were cast regardless. Less than two years after my registration there, a friend offered to take me to an audition for a new variety show assembled by Christophe Isard, a risk-taking TV producer looking for fresh talent. At the time, he ran the research section of the *Office de Radiodiffusion-Télévision Française*.

I'm not sure why I agreed to go. No doubt I didn't want to argue with that friend of mine. But this incident brings up my own ambivalence. On the one hand, my dream was to "succeed in music." On the other, I was doing absolutely nothing to make that happen. My real goal, like that of Julius Cesar who claimed to prefer being the first consul of a second-rate city than the second consul of Rome, was to become a third-class singer, who would wander his life away in an anecdotal notoriety. It was never star status that attracted me. What I envisioned was being a singer-songwriter with enough recognition to figure somewhere on the palette of French song – what we called then *la nouvelle chanson française*, to distinguish it from pop dreck. My dream was to record an album. But I didn't want to get up on stage.

In fact, the idea scared the shit out of me.

The day of the audition, the hall was enormous and full of about a hundred hopefuls from all corners of France. It was the first time I participated in an operation like this, or even witnessed one. An astonishing spectacle. Four-fifths of those brave young souls dared to offer something that one had to ask oneself, when they started up, if it were third-degree burlesque, or if their innocence was at the level of delirium. Saccharine words like stale rosewater, or on the contrary, ridiculous attempts at political engagement, melodies we'd all heard five thousand times, always with the same three chords on barely tuned guitars, all carried on bleating voices, cracking falsely, twisted falsettos and howling tenors. It was pathetic, but it also put me at ease. I'd always found my songs flawed and my voice a little false.

When my turn came, I played two songs, the first of which, "José le rat," is a sort of homage to "my" Saint-Sébastien's Dead End and the weirdos that populated it. "José le rat," later rebaptised "Chicago-Montreuil," hit the target. I saw some genuinely appreciative smiles cross the faces of Isard and his team. They didn't seem to hear the defects in the song, or to begrudge my voice.

They signed me for a broadcast. I was going to be on TV! Like The Beatles or Chantal Goya! Were the paths to glory opening before me? The broadcast would be called: "Through the Big Door."

A few days later I was headed to a studio on the edge of the Parc des Buttes-Chaumont in a polka dot dress shirt, ready to get in front the cameras. I was running late, so I hailed a taxi. The driver recognized me, I recognized the driver. It's an old friend from high school, Michel Grossi. When I explained my destination and the reason I was going there, Grossi said, "You're going to be on TV? That's great. I hope it brings you luck in your career, happening to stumble into my cab." And he refused to let me pay the fare. That touched me. But I don't believe that a "career" depends on good or bad luck, much less on simple desire.

The day of the broadcast, my friend Nyger, who had a big TV (I didn't have one) invited me over with a group of friends. We sat there silently on his sofa with a bowl of peanuts and watched Sébastien Régnier with his polka dot shirt and his long hair. I had the impression of being split in two.

Viewers seemed to like it, so Isard hired me for a second broadcast, then for a third. Being on TV became something of a habit, and I became the star of the Dead End.

One day, Anne-Marie Grosjean, Isard's assistant, called me to tell me that I'd been selected to participate in "la tournée des nouveaux espoirs de la chanson française," a tour of the rising stars of French song. The headliner of the show was Yves Simon. The others were all unknowns, except for a certain Hervé Cristiani, who'd already recorded an album on Polydor. There was also Marie-José Vilar, a resolutely uptown girl with a taste for booze (my sister in this respect), but very talented and nice. And then there was Roland Magdane who was at the time into a kind of mustachioed and politicized romanticism, before converting himself a few years later into a stand-up comic. The tour was filmed, from beginning to end, for a TV broadcast the following summer. At a meeting in preparation for the tour, one of the directors, Claude Massot, was introduced to us. Our departure was preceded by a cocktail party. When we climbed on board the bus, I had the impression of embarking on the "Magical Mystery Tour."

It was a fucking bordello in the hotels we stayed at, and we played all the biggest venues – which turned out to be a grave strategic error. Since nobody'd ever heard of us, those big halls were three-quarters empty. That didn't prevent me from having stagefright; I ended up getting pickled before every show, and my performance suffered badly from it. Isard wasn't happy and he let me have it. He took a risk in signing all of us, and he wouldn't stand for the tour to be ruined by badly timed benders.

Isard also tried to teach me another lesson, which has stayed with me all my life but which I've never learned to follow: "Stop writing new songs, Sébastien! You should just concern yourself with the ones you've already written, polish them, learn them, practice them!" But what's to be done, the song-making machine just won't stop. I still can't hold them back.

If that tour didn't lead to anything concrete for me, it certainly wasn't in vain. It gave me two friends for life, and now for death, Claude Massot and Hervé Cristiani.

Hervé was a fingerpicking ace, and a beast on stage despite being no more than twenty-five. With our mutual enthusiasm for weed, we became inseparable on the tour, and we always got dibs on the seats at the back of the bus, where we could calmly roll ourselves a spliff and talk about the future. Those were definitive and decisive dialogues for me. I liked to say that the future floated before me in a haze, attracted as I was by a thousand contradictory things, by travels first and foremost, but also by painting, photography… And perfumes, why not? I had in my head a notion of a cultural object which would take the form of a box containing sounds, images, scents, a little vial of an elixir… A voyage for the senses.

Hervé didn't see things that way. "Me, I only know how to do one thing: to sing and write songs. I'm obliged to do that and succeed at it, I have no choice!"

No choice, maybe that's the key. Result: Hervé crossed the threshold, while I spent my life in a long half-hearted flirt with life. That lasted for decades. I made my travels, my paintings, he recorded his albums, we'd meet regularly, I'd tell him about my adventures and we'd listen to each other's new songs, because of course I didn't stop making those too. Except that his songs were recorded on vinyl. Hervé always loved what I wrote and couldn't understand why I didn't do anything with it. He always supported me, encouraged me, connected me as best he could. Until one day, twenty years later, he shook his head and said to me, "Yours, my old man, is going to be posthumous."

But back then, feeling obliged, and with the occasional kick in the ass by Hervé, I'd occasionally play small clubs where illustrious forebears had their start (Brassens, Brel…), places that were the necessary rite of passage for any singer just starting out. For the most part, it consisted of pushing past the clatter of forks, plates and conversation. A battery of blows raining down every time.

But a few strange things also happened. One evening at the American Center, which was the launch pad for all the young anti-variety folksingers, I played my little set (three songs maximum), and the crowd reacted in a truly unexpected and enthusiastic fashion. They demanded more. After the second encore, the organizer dragged me off the stage. But the audience wouldn't let go of me, buying me beers and giving me my fifteen minutes of glory.

A more somber memory: *La vieille grille*. Without a doubt the most watched cabaret on the Left Bank of Paris. I scored a gig there. If it worked out, I'd be contracted to play there for two or three weeks, for good money. I just had to make it through five or six songs...

I didn't make it. Even though I'd stuffed the place with buddies of mine, when I found myself on stage, with the lights in my eyes and my pals invisible in the dark, and in the middle of the second song, I hit the hole, the ravine, the gulf. No way to remember the next word. Instead of improvising, noodling away like anybody else would have done, I sat there, mute, for about twenty seconds, motionless on the stage, in a sepulchral silence, before serenely packing up my guitar and ducking out the back door of the club.

My visits to record labels were hardly any better. At the time, selling songs to producers meant picking up your guitar and going to sing in their offices. You didn't even send a tape, that came after.

I didn't like producers, and they didn't seem to think much better of me. In general, they wore their shirts open, exposing hairy chests and gold chains. They looked to me like a bunch of pimps. Anyway, that's the reason I gave myself to repeatedly blow my chances.

My behavior was something between incoherence and arrogance. Every time I was led to the door. On my way, all I ever managed to get was a critique of my voice. They suggested that I take a few singing lessons, and that pissed me off even more. Did Dylan take singing lessons?

Marie-José Vilar, whom I still saw sometimes, had just gotten a three-album deal. Very generously, she offered to throw me a crumb, getting me a meeting with her producer. She really believed in my songs and she, too, found it perplexing that I couldn't find a home for them. She insisted on going to the meeting with me, saying, "I want to understand what's going on."

Leaving the meeting, she told me: "Now I understand." First, I'd give the guy every argument to undermine what I was doing: "I'm warning you, it's not really finished, it's too high for my voice, I need to work on the lyrics…" Then, according to Marie-José: "The real use you make of your guitar is to hide behind it!"

I'd also gotten close to Camille, Marie-José's guitarist. A sort of romantic skeleton with a burning gaze and waist-length hair. A total Hendrix addict. On the stage, he played with his back turned to the audience so they couldn't see what he was up to next. I loved that. And his left hand was a nervous spider running up and down the fretboard, and his spirit was ultra-rock. A real stoner to boot.

Camille had a bassist friend, Maurice, AKA Momo. With another buddy who was a percussionist, they came to visit me on the Dead End, and over a case of beers, we decided to form a band: Naja. The repertoire would be my songs. Our practice studio: the cellar of the bistro downstairs. We practiced, it worked, we scored a couple of gigs at the *Maison des Jeunes et de la Culture*, the House of Youth and Culture, and it seemed to go all right. As long as I wasn't alone on stage, things went better. And it was great to be part of a group! To break our backs lugging around the amps!

The problem was that Naja was made up of total lushes. It took place mostly in a comatose state. The whole thing vanished into thin air.

I eked out a living giving guitar lessons. For somebody who always judged himself a limited guitarist, that might sound like a stretch. But I know something about the instrument, the fretboard, inversions, plus in that period I worked to pick up some of Dadi's and Leo Kottke's fingerpicking techniques (aided by open tuning), such that I could offer a basic introduction to beginning guitarists.

And then, the last benefit of that "tour of the rising stars of French song": a little delivery of unanticipated cash. One day, I passed by the SACEM headquarters, by chance. A pretty good sum was waiting for me there, payment on my songwriter rights. SACEM then was located on the rue Chaptal, in Pigalle. To get the metro from there, I passed by the Victor Flore Music Store. Looking at the store window – love at first sight. The guitar of my dreams was in there, with its tag marked "Like New – On Sale." I went in and askd the price, which was in the ball park of the check I just received. Five minutes later, I could barely contain my joy, stepping out on the street, without a dime left in my pocket, but the proud owner of a Martin D18. The guitar of Donovan, among others. A guitar whose legend will only grow with the years. That was in '74. She's never abandoned me. Nor I her.

All that made of my youth a floating revery, fed with music and dreams, and drowned in alcohol.

One year later, my baldness already well advanced, I suddenly got a call.

"I'd like to speak with Sébastien Régner."

"That's me."

"Oh, hey! I don't know if you remember me, we were together at Voltaire. Frédérique Tchékovich, does that mean anything to you?"

That really threw me for a loop. What could he want from me? How had he gotten my number?

"I got your number from the phone book. Could we see each other one of these days?"

We saw each other. He'd changed. In fact, it was a metamorphosis. Gone was the little dandy, pink and pinched. I saw before me a bearded philosophy student, relaxed and wearing glasses. His hair was still long, but sticking out in every direction. He was wearing jeans and a blue sweater. He was living with his girlfriend, Eve, also a student, and to my eyes they seemed like the perfect couple. Without irony. It looked to me like everything was going well for them. Nice little apartment on the boulevard Voltaire, and in the corner, next to his Gibson Les Paul, a Revox recording system that I was eyeing. He offered me some tea, distracting me from my curiosity. I couldn't imagine what he wanted from me.

He told me he was impressed with my reputation as a lyricist and a "song factory." He'd heard about that, and he stored it in some corner of his head, and it came back to him, as if it were natural, four years later. In sum, he proposed a collaboration. He wanted to read some of my texts, to listen to my songs.

I served him my musical soup, and when we left each other an hour and a half later, it was with a moral contract in our pockets. We'd make a demo tape together and show it to some labels. With his playing and my songs, everything polished up on his Magic Revox.

The four-track Revox, that was the ancestor of the home recording studio. Super sound quality and the possibility of layering tracks by re-recording, passing from one to two, and back to one, etc... After the fourteenth pass or so, it started to sound a little fried, but it was doable. Freddy was lucky enough to own one, and I was lucky enough that he wanted to keep it at my place.

All of a sudden, with the reappearance of Freddy, some form of discipline came into my life, full-force. With him, there was no question of leaving anything to chance. Freddy didn't drink, he didn't smoke, he didn't do drugs. He defined our work schedule and from then on, we worked every day from 2:00 to 4:00 in the afternoon, putting together our demo tape. And if I had a hangover or was five mintues late, he made me pay with the kind of scathing remarks you'd use to scold a naughty kid. It was real work. And each time our session ended, he'd go back to his life, me to mine.

In a few weeks, two months maybe, we'd laid down about fifteen tracks, a great little demo with some careful arrangements, maybe a bit too careful in fact. As a bonus, thanks to a quirky producer who was a fan of my songs, we scored a studio session to really polish up the lead track: *"Cent Balles."* We called in some musicians, among them Richard Kolinka with his drums. Some beautiful water had flowed under the bridge since Richard's high school days. He was a respected drummer, and what a drummer! He was playing with a really promising group called Téléphone. Freddy had been part of the original nucleus of the band, when it was a little outfit called Semolina.

Honestly, I can't remember if we ever showed anybody our tape. Weirdly, Freddy seemed to leave it up to me, apparently convinced that I was already well-installed in the world of show biz.

But all that wasn't for naught. The experience brought us together on a human level. Something that didn't want to say its name, above all not the name of friendship, and yet it had the color and the smell of it. Humor was what stuck us together – I'd make him laugh though he didn't want to show it, and that made me laugh though I didn't want to show it, and that, that was really funny, like a code between the two of us.

One of the rare times when we saw each other

outside of work hours, I wanted to verify one thing. I asked him to hypnotize me. He hesitated a little, saying that he wasn't doing that any longer, then he accepted. As I predicted, it didn't work.

But in a completely unexpected way from such a secretive guy, somebody so disinclined to personal chit-chat, Freddy began to to open up to me about very intimate things, which helped me to at least partially pierce his mystery. Family stories are really not my cup of tea. But this one was worth the detour. That was the heyday of the anti-psychiatric movement: Laing, Cooper, Ken Loach's *Family Life*... Except that for Freddy, none of that was theoretical – it was based on lived experience.

He'd grown up among his father, his mother, his brother and his sister. Which might have been a little circle of perfect happiness. But that wasn't the case. For reasons of economic precarity, he'd had to share a single bedroom with his brother and sister (both older than him) for years. Well, in the course of those years, his sleep had been accompanied by rales of animal cries, mixed in the shadows, as his brother fornicated with his sister against her will, night after night. That sinister, hellish practice went on until his sister tried to escape through marriage. But his brother couldn't accept it and was determined to keep up his idylle by any means necessary. So his sister found another escape: suicide. His brother fled, disappearing forever.

The only ones left were Freddy's mother and father. An adoring mother, a father in slippers. Napoleon was his name. In his little empire, he wandered from his yard to his arm chair, from his arm chair to his yard, in striped pajamas. Struck by a sort of irreversible neurasthenia. The mother compensated with a kind of permanent overactivity, maintaining her devastated little cell with constant housekeeping. Her exemplary cleanliness masked the pestilent drama. She polished, scrubbed, shined everything, taking care of her vegetable husband as if he were a child. And she adored Freddy. Probably the only kid she ever should have had.

That tells you how much Freddy considered me an intimate. First because he'd confided in me this nightmarish story, as a means of justifying his profound disgust toward the notion of family in general, and his in particular. But even more astonishing to me was that one day, under the pretext of going to pick up some clothes, he asked me to go along with him to his parents' house, on the rue du Chemin Vert. Which had always been forbidden territory for his friends in high school.

When his mother opened the door, it was Moses opening the tabernacle. The light of God filled her and lit up her face, discovering her son on the welcome mat. Not even a glance for me, everything for her beloved child there before her, popping by without advance notice, and it was a sort of neurotic transe. We slipped on shoe covers, I saw Napoleon in his arm chair, Freddy submitted to a ritual of eating a plate of cookies surrounded by the smells of cleaning products and the doting admiration from his mother. And then we got the hell out of there.

After we'd made that demo, Freddy left the Revox for a while at my house. In the evening, in the shadows of my digs at the terminus of the Dead End, I shut myself up with my guitar and my dog, and I recorded the blues, making sure to have wrecked my voice beforehand by smoking a pack of Gauloises. Mississippi John Hurt took his place of honor. Jazz Gillum too, and Big Bill Broonzy.

A little later that year, another call from Freddy. He had a plan. To quickly put together a group for a gig at the Club Med. Flirting with girls under the Tunisian sun on the princess's bankroll, providing the nightly dance music for tacky couples, fed, lodged and paid for our services... That was the dream gig for third-rate bands of the time.

We found ourselves in a basement studio rehearsing like madmen and without proper introductions to each other. The repertoire? Everything playing on the radio, but to keep ourselves entertained, we added a few of our favorite pearls, The Beatles, The Stones. After a few sessions we had a version of "Lady Madonna" that sounded as good as the original... But all of it burst like a soap bubble when Club Med passed on our services.

A few months later, I'm the one who contacted Freddy. The half-baked producer of "La Flûte d'Israël" had called me about a new record, destined for the supermarkets... A project worse than airport Muzak. But maybe something could come of it. I thought Freddy and I could offer him something. This time, I found Freddy with a shaved head, and separated from Eve. Me too, I'd shaved my head a few years earlier, in high school. He told me he'd been impressed by that. "So, Régnier! I see you can find no middle ground!," my math teacher said at the time.

We picked up the Revox again and got to work making some facile music. But with his soaring guitar riffs, it suddenly started to sound like something. A few days later we were in a studio for twelve hours straight, recording a dozen tracks. The mixing helped, and we were pretty happy with the results. This time it's better than a tape on the shelf, it's a 33 1/3 that I still have a copy of in my attic. But above all, thanks to the cash we got, I was able to buy my own Revox.

A sort of poisonous gift. I become engulfed for a few years, recording songs, always in the form of demos, always with the idea of presenting them to producers. But I spent so much time hoping to give them the final, polishing touches, and I got so much onanistic pleasure from it (I actually came once in the middle of a fifth take on a guitar part), never mind all the new songs that I kept writing, that I had no time left to show anyone.

That was '75. Between Freddy and me, it was the start of a new eclipse.

Chapter 7
Virus

As I said, I'm not sure what we learned, or what we left behind, on the Eastern European Tour. But something seemed to follow us home. When Imre was back in Normandy and I was in New York, I got an email ostensibly emanating from somebody named "Olga":

> How do you do,
> It is Olga and i like to talk with you!
> I received your e-mail thru a dating bureau so i came out with an idea,
> why don't i write a letter to you ;)
> I am intended to find a nice buddy, a man, perhaps a boyfriend.
> Yes, i used to talk about love and erotic themes straightly and
> i don't like any tricks, it's all so simple :),
> so if you don't mind we could use this opportunity to talk a little
> and send some photos to each other, maybe some naked pictures either?! ;)
> Anyway, if you are even just a little interested, please mail me to my
> e-mail: simple.dance@gmx.net
> I want to believe that you considered my thoughts being interesting and

you'll reply soon!
many sweet kisses,
Olga

Perhaps I don't need to tell you that I was not registered with any "dating bureau." It appeared that this same email had gone out to any number of users of my employer's server, as well as that of AOL. I thought that was funny, so I forwarded the message to Imre. A minute later, I thought better of it, and quickly sent another message saying, "Imre! Don't click on the link!"

Too late. Since it was being forwarded from me, he didn't think twice about the possible consequences, and he fell hook line and sinker for "Olga"'s trick. Soon pop up ads were flashing all over his screen, with GIFs of seductive Eastern European girls waggling their bosoms and winking at him. It was a few weeks before his next visit, when I took him to the Apple Store to have somebody at the Genius Bar clean everything up for him.

Later I wrote some lyrics about the Olga debacle, which Imre set to music, describing the forwarded flirtation and the nasty virus that ensued. To write the words, I basically just copied her email, slightly rearranging things to get some rhymes in, and I made up a little commentary from Imre's perspective, mostly in French, but adding the suspicious observation, "Her English it is weird. / This message just appeared / This morning in my mail out of the blue." Of course, that phrase, "her English it is weird," was a friendly little tease about the minor grammatical errors and ideosyncracies that pop up when one speaks or writes in a foreign language. The gentle poke could be understood as being aimed at "Olga," but possibly Imre as well. In fact, as I said, his spoken English is extremely fluent, as is his written English, though it's true that it includes some sentences clearly structured on the basis of French grammar, and he occasionally translates French idiomatic expressions directly, with slightly comical results. So now, when this happens, I smile and say, "Your English it is weird."

But of course, it takes some nerve for me to say this, because my French it is REALLY weird. And, in fact, though I call this a "tease" and "poke," in truth, I love the strange poetry that arises in translingual communications. I'm translating Imre's French into English in this narrative, but I sort of wish he were telling all of his story in his quirky, Lodbroggish version of American vernacular speech, which is largely the language he uses with me day-to-day. It's so charming.

And I'm also not immune to the charms of "Olga"'s prose, or that of the various non-native speakers of English who contact me on a regular basis. I seem to get more of these messages than most. I'm not just talking about the regular scams from ostensible international sheiks and princes who want to send me a heap of cash if I'll just kindly supply them with my bank account information. I get a lot of messages that are sincerely directed to me — and some that may be sincere, though it's hard to tell.

Many are inquiries from far-flung scholars or artists who want to study with me, either in my capacity as a dance specialist, or more generally, as a theorist of performance. Here's an approximation of one I received recently. I hope you will understand that it's quite possible that the author is a very bright person and maybe a thinker and/or performer of great originality.

Sweetness greetings. I am Lin Hwang or
somebody call me just Happy Hwang.
I am a dreamful girl, live and well in Taiwan
great beautiful!
I have masterful of ideas to the performance art.
I am really
big ambition to get in to new york university.
I will remain willingful to be study with you
excellent teacher. Nonetheless impossible almost,
rooting for me be please. My email though could
you have feeling of longwinded thank you not
giving up for me.
Never give up!
In my right mind, I urgency to keep effort of
reaching you, I'll keep going my toil evermore to
get in your school.
I'll send mail constantly. Please remember me.

I found those last two lines in particular simultaneously extremely poignant and a little terrifying.

I responded to this inquiry as I often do, saying I looked forward to reading her application, and in fact, she never wrote back. But the promise of persistence struck a chord, because in fact, some of my foreign correspondents have been pretty dogged in their determination.

There was, for example, Massahoud Cherif. Well, that's actually an imaginary name, which is to say, I made it up by looking up the most common given and surnames in Mauritania, which was ostensibly the homeland of my correspondent, who went by another name, which may or may not have been fictitious. I received the first message from Cherif several months ago, and even among the inquiries I field from international dance enthusiasts, this one seemed a little strange:

Hello madam, my name is
Massahoud, I am Mauritania but I left my
country for political reasons and I live
in xxxxxxx for five years. I am 32 years old and
I am passionate about all forms of classical
and modern dance and also ritual. When
I was younger, I watched the movie several
times, this is what inspired me. But in my
country, I have not been able to practice as a man
dancing is considered a homosexual. I married
a xxxxian woman to obtain a residence permit,
but I never had sex with her and we parted. My
ambition is to one day go to the United States is a
free country and where I could practice
my passion. I work in a specialized video shop
and I've been an actor in specialized films make
money, but it does not match my tastes. My father
is a very rich man who is willing to helpme but I
do not like to ask. I want to know the
dances related to sexual and ritual practices in
different civilizations. Can you advise me on
this and give mesome personal advice? I will be
very grateful if you answer me on this subject
that fascinates me greatly and would have an
exchange. Thank you.

Massahoud Cherif

It sounded a little fishy, but you never know, and I
didn't want to be dismissive if in fact Massahoud Cherif
was truly interested in global dance, so I answered:

Hi Massahoud. Here's a list of some of the texts
I teach in my dance ethnography course. On
the topic of sexuality and dance, you might be
particularly interested in Marta Savigliano's work
on tango, and Fiona Buckland on queer club
dance. Best of luck, B

Franziska Boas et al., The Function of Dance in
Human Society; Marcel Mauss,Techniques of the
Body ; Maya Deren, Divine Horsemen; Katherine
Dunham, Island Possessed; Cynthia
Novack, Sharing the Dance; Sally Ann
Ness, Body, Movement, and Culture; Barbara
Browning, Samba: Resistance in Motion; Marta
Savigliano, Tango and the Political Economy
of Passion; Julie Taylor, Paper Tangos; Fiona
Buckland, Impossible Dance

By the way, sorry for the immodesty of including my
own book in that bibliography, but indeed, if one were
looking for some readable texts to begin one's studies
in dance cultures, this list wouldn't be a bad place to
start.

Massahoud seemed to appreciate the direction:

Thank you for your
answering Madam Browning, you meet my

expectations. My life is directed towards the experience of erotic dance ritual. I will try to see this books. I have very fond of tango because it's like love acting in dance. My job pays me well and also in relation to sex but I never have a role where I can dance. I would like to find one opportunity to do this work with dancing too. I have a technical skill for it I think. But I do not have a feminine partner. My girlfriend works in the same profession as me and she told me to forget the erotic dance to develop my other skills. Is it possible to get private lessons on the internet ? I do not have the ability to send you a video. I can send you a picture but I do not show my face on the internet because of my job. Maybe we can exchange in the future about this dances. And thank you for the books I will try to find.

Massahoud

It was getting a little weird. I didn't answer this one, and perhaps you can see why. That didn't seem to discourage Massahoud, who wrote again the next day:

Dear madam Browning, as you suggested, i have order the Marta Savigliano book on the amazon. I hope you can have some video demonstration for me performing your skills in tango so i can work my part. i can understand if you do not accept to show your face. I would like to go out my job and my gril friend to become a dancer. thank you for encouraging me. Do you want i send you a picture but i cannot show my face in the

internet, also because my family in mauritania. I have many regards to you.
Massahoud

My first thought was, oh no, what if Massahoud starts writing to Marta Savigliano and tells her I sent him? But the even more disconcerting thing was that he seemed to think I might want to send him a more or less erotic dance video with my head cropped out.

The disconcerting part was not just that that was such an inappropriate suggestion. It was also that, if a person actually knew me, they might in fact think it was a pretty *reasonable* suggestion. You may remember that I mentioned some artistic videos that had been screened in the bathroom that night of my first show with Imre. The ones I said might be construed, depending on one's taste, as either "lyrical and uncanny, or baffling and mildly obscene." Well. If you'd seen them, you might actually think Massahoud's entreaty was not entirely out of the range of possibility.

Of course, when I make a dance video, it's certainly not instructional, nor to my mind pornographic, and my own reading of my work (again, I apologize if this sounds immodest) tends toward "lyrical and uncanny" rather than "obscene." But as we know, obscenity is in the eye of the beholder.

I really didn't want to encourage Massahoud, so I thought I'd try sending a final message that was professional, curt and conclusive:

Sorry, I can only advise you on the academic end of things. Best of luck. B

But it seems he was not so easy to deter. He answered:

> Dear madam Browning, i like very much an academic. I thinks it was what makes serious about erotic ritual dances i want to perform and learn. I expect this very much from you because you are the good person to teach me, what i want to learn and get passion with my skills. Thank you for helping and willing
> Massahoud

Obviously, the only option at this point was radio silence. Still, after twenty-four hours, Massahoud gave it one last college try:

> Dear Madam Browning, i understand you do not answer because you are too famous teacher and too much requests. I will try make my way dancing and meeting a chance to perform my skills. because i want to change my specilaised job and go to my passion of erotic ritual dances. thank your for your advise in the book and if you want i can send you a photo souvenir from Massahoud in last mail. But i will not tell my girlfriend who is jealous mistress. Best regards.
> Massahoud Cherif

Needless to say, I didn't request a photo.

All of this may strike you as a sort of comical conundrum, but in truth, it freaked me out a little, because it came on the heels of a very disturbing episode demonstrating the possible pitfalls of correspondence and collaboration on the Internet. As you know, the ether of that space was where Imre and I first met, but ours was not my first long-distance collaboration. About a year before "Browning," I'd had contact with another person who was posting musical files online. One of them seemed to me entirely unique — a virtuosic ukulele interpretation of Paganini's "Caprice in A Minor: Tema con Variazioni (Quasi Presto)." I contacted the poster, asking permission to make a dance to it, a proposition that this person happily accepted.

This led to a long and intense exchange of text, sound and video files, as well as the manuscript of a novel, which combusted quite suddenly when my collaborator was exposed by other online musicians as having pilfered and digitally altered the sound files of others. Which led to the further revelation that the personal information communicated in our correspondence had also been a work of fiction.

I should perhaps be embarrassed to say that I took this fiction for reality, going so far as to arrange a meeting with my correspondent in this person's purported city, in a country in which I knew no one, the language of which I didn't speak. Of course, when I got there, my collaborator failed to materialize, and surely any normal person would have gotten the picture. But I didn't. I accepted a highly suspect explanation for this humiliating fiasco. Was it because I was so excited about the artistic collaboration that I persisted in believing in it? That seems to be the most logical explanation. Anyway, it was only after others supplied the irrefutable evidence that I finally acknowledged to myself what had happened.

I tried to be philosophical about it. After all, I had, and have, a vested interest in considering the blurry boundary between reality and fiction. Except that in my own case, I'm perhaps absurdly compelled to point out the difference, and the places where I alter the "facts." Why do I place that word in inverted commas? Because any two-bit psychoanalyst will tell you that our representations of the "realities" of our lives are heavily influenced by the stories we all want to tell ourselves about who we are.

But as you'll notice, I've told you when I've changed some names or other identifying factors in this narrative out of discretion, as in the cases of Lin Hwang and Massahoud Cherif. As well as Natalija Dombrovska and Boriss Gruba.

I also readily admit to augmenting the intrigue around those last two. In truth, the individuals on which they're based are no more Boris and Natasha-style villains (this time in the guise of neo-liberal corporate productivity experts) than any other moderately conservative workaday businesspeople trying to adapt to the global political changes of the last twenty-five years. And now I'll tell you that they weren't, in fact, even responsible for that little tiff that Imre and I had in Klaipéda. The disturbing and mysterious text that I received about an anarchist code name had nothing to do with them. It was in fact from one of these other Internet musicians, in the aftermath of the pilfered sound files mess. It was trying to warn me that my plagiarist collaborator was back on the scene, under a new false persona.

Maybe you can understand why this whole story

irked Imre. The exposure of the plagiarist occurred just as Imre and I were beginning our own artistic association. He was a little befuddled by my naiveté, and impatient with my distraction by this fraud, when we so clearly had real work to do. I agreed that it was time to move on, but it wasn't quite so easy to extricate myself from that story, which spawned a terrifying chapter in which one of the other musicians who had collaborated with the plagiarist determined, mistakenly, that I was behind the whole scam. He freaked out and started sending me all manner of accusatory and chilling messages, appearing to believe that my interest in semi-fiction indicated not a desire to lay bare my own writerly process, but rather to play some kind of evil puppet-master role, manipulating unsuspecting individuals as I roped them into my bogus world.

The onslaught of accusations was pretty traumatizing. Also, in an effort to *really* lay bare the extent to which I'd believed in the story myself, I'd sent the guy the manuscript of my novel, and links to the collaborative videos I'd made with this fictional artist, believing him to be real. Precisely the ones screened in the bathroom at my first show with Imre.

It was immediately after that performance, in fact, that, as the saying goes, the shit hit the fan. As you can perhaps imagine, sharing that material was a bad idea. But I was so disoriented, my judgment was a little impaired. It was like quicksand – every effort to extract myself seemed to drag me further in. When Massahoud popped up, I even, perhaps paranoidly, thought it might be an effort to exact revenge against manipulations mistakenly attributed to me.

All of this is to say, if it wasn't already obvious to you, that collaboration via digital files on the Internet can be *at least* as fraught as going head-to-head together with somebody in a studio. Though in some cases, as in the story between Imre and me, collaboration at a distance can lead quite magically to something else altogether.

So, Imre can get a little touchy about that whole story. At one point, he too was fielding messages from that accusatory guy, who'd progressed to contacting my intimates, including my former lover. I don't even know how he tracked her down. Needless to say, she was also none too pleased.

But Imre's not without his own experiences of sticky or even tragic correspondence and collaboration, both on- and offline. Still, since I'm talking in this chapter about online misadventures, I'll just mention a couple of those. There was a woman who really dug his music and asked to meet him in Paris. He thought it was about the music, but she pulled an excellent bottle of wine out of the trunk of her car and invited him immediately to her hotel room. He politely declined. There was somebody else who kept sending him messages on SoundCloud about when she was ovulating, saying she liked to masturbate to his tunes. All of this flummoxed him.

There were a few other people who genuinely seemed interested in collaborating with him – some fingerpickers of his generation that dug his sound, and several singers, Dombrovska included, who asked to record covers of his originals. And then there were those who just wrote to express enthusiasm, and a few people to whom Imre wrote to express, in his turn, appreciation of their artistry.

But even this could prove complicated. The most heartbreaking story involved a young singer/songwriter in Scandinavia, a woman with a wistful voice and a simple but lovely guitar technique. I'll call her Nyx, the name of a lunar goddess. Hers was something like that. He alerted me to her, thinking I might share his regard for her body of work, and I did. Her songs were all quite similar – as Imre put it, seemingly one long, quiet, plaintive cry. Why were they so affecting? Aside from the native loveliness of her voice, I can only explain the appeal through their unmistakable sincerity.

She had almost no followers at all. Imre felt compelled to encourage her, and soon she left him a couple of messages of gratitude, which quickly became a little frightening, as she communicated in them some of the same despair and hopelessness that ran through her songs. When she appeared to desire from Imre encouragement that went beyond the question of music, he worried she might be expecting more engagement than he felt he could offer, and he pulled back. Maybe she looked for this support from other strangers, or maybe from her friends, and maybe, for some reason or another, it was never enough. But after a time, she stopped posting music, and Imre wondered what had happened.

After Nyx disappeared, Imre worried about her. Despite his usual disinclination to Google anything, he did a bit of his own Internet sleuthing and discovered the sad truth, if you think the trail of online postings and a Facebook page with her same avatar might be an indication of a reliable "true" story. Nyx had posted a number of seemingly delusional comments indicating that a Danish pop star had stolen one of her songs, and then that her family was trying to make her take anti-psychotic medications, and then that she was being locked up, and finally it appeared, from the mix of heartbroken and angry comments of others, that she had taken her own life.

I thought of Nyx when Imre later told me the story of the delicate young pianist he'd met at the Ecole Normale de Musique. Or maybe I thought of the pianist when we pieced together the story of Nyx. Right now I can't remember which came first, both stories are so sad.

Chapter 8
Contagion

IN '76, I got some work picking cherries in Ardèche, and I fell in love with the farmer's daughter, Renée. She saved me from the Dead End, both figuratively and literally. Everything happened very fast, we met, we got on well, we got married for fun, and at the age of twenty-five, I become a father. Tom, a little blonde moppet I believed I'd already seen in a dream. Renée shared my taste for travel. From time to time, we left our son with his grandmother in Ardèche and we hit the road. Nepal, India, and in '81, the whole little family took off for three months in Sri Lanka.

The system consisted of working in Paris and setting aside enough cash to finance the next trip. But becoming the father of a family implied a social position that I hadn't imagined. One has to account for oneself. One day, an austere stranger knocked on our door. She's a social worker, and she began her interrogation: What are your sources of income, etc.

Obviously, they were my private guitar lessons, and a few little housepainting jobs I'd rounded up (and even some carpentry gigs!). All of that money was under the table, and I hadn't been paying any income tax. The good woman told me sternly: "You do not fit in my forms!" I tried to explain that I was a musician, that I made do, with the occasional help of my parents, but that didn't satisfy her. Now that I was a dad, it was time to get my life in order. And what she proposed was to help me find a job, one that would leave my weekends free so I could practice my music too. What a brilliant idea! Why hadn't I thought of it myself? I swallowed my tongue. But seeing that I bristled, the good woman began to brandish some not very veiled threats, like, for example, "We'll take the kid away from you." That was too much. I threw her out and, thank God, she never came back. Me, thirty years later, I still wouldn't fit in her forms.

Meanwhile, most of my time, it was about my songs. I spent days and days glued to the good old Revox, exploring new paths, new sounds, adding to my guitars some other instruments gathered here and there, a rhythm box, and a little contraption that will become the legendary Moog synthesizer, popularized by Harrison on his album *Electronic Sounds*. The tracks piled up. Music remained my obsession, my dream. I put together a new band with Jean-Charles, a doctor friend. With his advice, I managed to get a great deal on an old black Telecaster, the second guitar of my life, for all of my life. We recorded a demo tape, in the damp cellar of a club called "Splendid." We were up to our ankles in water – the amps and wires too. Jean-Charles really believed in it. Music was more than his dream, it was his pressure relief valve. We were into JJ Cale, Dire Straits. I'd written a slew of songs in this spirit. But all that starts to stall. Rehearsals were canceled, postponed, sometimes it was my fault…

When suddenly – a call. A scratchy voice: "It's Freddy!" He popped up again after an absence of six years. He had a few things to tell me and he invited me for a weekend at a cabin that somebody's lent him, and where he'd been spending some time with Zouzou, his new girlfriend. I went there. A new metamorphosis. Cowboy boots, sideburns, a tight little shirt. The guy seemed animalized. Nervous, wild, determined. Determined to do what? How? He was thirsty for glory and revenge. "I won't be satisfied until I have a wall of amps behind me and a sea of listeners in front of me!"

Me, I said it's about time. It's about time for this great talent to burst out before an audience. His guitar playing had reached the level of madness. Because for all these years, he'd kept working, working, working, torturing that fretboard.

The revenge he wanted? On himself, but above all, on Téléphone. Back in high school, a band had formed – a powerful rock trio with Freddy as the frontman, Daniel Roux on bass and Richard Kolinka on drums.

I'd suggested their first band name – Semolina – and it was the seed of what would become Téléphone. I don't know too much about why Freddy left the group, but I imagine that, already infected with megalomania, he slammed the door behind him, saying he wouldn't bet a kopeck on the group's direction, which must have seemed too commercial to him, being, as he was, a die-hard no-compromise kind of guy. What followed, we know. Téléphone became a hexagonal rock phenomenon, our own little Stones, shockingly successful: the first album went gold, the second platinum, exploding all over the covers of the rock 'n' roll magazines. And Freddy was left nowhere, ruminating in his bitterness. He couldn't swallow that, and at the time, in '81, he figured he could still show them. He'd put together his own group, with a name that augured a pandemic: Contagion.

Freddy was never one to talk just for talking's sake, and aside from music, he derided pretty much everything. Beginning with my private life. When I announced that I'd gotten married and had a kid, he barely reacted. That didn't interest him. Contagion had already recorded a first album with modest distribution, and a second was being mixed. He asked me to listen to it and he wanted to know what I think. I had two hesitations – first, the quality of the texts of the songs he showed me. On this point I've always been a self-avowed pain in the ass. But what really bothered me, and kept getting in the way of my listening, is that this bonehead Freddy, in putting together a rock group, instead of letting his amazing guitars finally explode, had chosen to mix them almost into the background, except for the rhythm guitar, which took over the whole sound. And the hellish solos that I'd been waiting ages to hear, to see etched into the grooves of an album, were reduced to a few mordant phrases, like scattered little tigers' fangs, short bursts – much too brief for my taste.

At the same time, I must confess that I admired the way he'd economized his talent, distributing it with parsimony. Anybody else in his place, and a lot of people with a lot less talent, would have fallen to the temptation of those long solos that signal the amateurism of so many groups. This guy played it straight. Still, the sound was pretty enormous. At that time, Freddy was deep into heavy metal, above all AC/DC. He pushed his voice to its upper limits, like Angus Young, and mixed everything to accentuate the medium and treble tones. The only apparent concession to the image of Téléphone was that he'd taken an ex-girlfriend, Léonie, as the bassist for the group. Téléphone also had a female bassist.

For his part, when he heard what I was doing with Jean-Charles, he didn't mince words: cat piss. I didn't agree, and I'll always prefer JJ Cale to AC/DC, but Freddy had a right to think what he wanted. And then suddenly he launched into one of his sermons about me, many more of which were still to come, some bordering on true delirium. The general idea was that I didn't know who I was. And, for that matter, what I was capable of. Once, when I was coming back from Lorraine just before an enormous gas explosion that claimed many victims, he clearly established a link between the incident with the fact of my having been nearby.

That weekend, while walking around a lake, Freddy proposed to me, without any warning, that I join

Contagion. It didn't make any sense, but I could smell a powder keg ready to blow. I said, "I'm in!"

Jean-Charles was really pissed off. And for my part, the adventure was risky. Contagion was already complete, they didn't need anybody: Freddy plus another excellent guitarist, Léo on the bass, and a super drummer. What was left for me to do? "You'll play keyboards," he told me. What keyboards? One week later, I was rehearsing with them in a studio on the rue Blanche, tethered to a Farfisa, the poor man's Hammond, along with my little Moog synthesizer. My former pianistic experience proved useful.

Freddy whipped his troops into shape. Ten hours of practice a day, going over the same bit twenty times. Léo had an advantage over the rest of us: she could sleep while playing, or, to be more accurate, play while sleeping. At first I thought it was just a meditative pose, but then I actually heard her snoring. The pace didn't change: it's every day, including weekends. After having been a bit suspicious in the beginning, the other members of Contagion seemed to adopt me.

Tiring but pleasurable. At the end of each session, we'd roll a massive joint, which Freddy wouldn't touch, and the rest of us would ramble on in dazed confusion until finally that diabolical guitarist laid into us. What a shame that we never recorded that!

The repertoire was violent. For the first time, I was practicing somebody else's songs, not my own. It was good for me. Even if, once in a while, I allowed myself to suggest changing a word or a comma here and there. I was the only one from whom Freddy would take any criticism. The studio next to ours was being rented by another group, led by Daniel Roux, the guy from Semolina. He'd also dropped out before the band became Téléphone, although he later found himself Aubert's bassist... before cracking his pipe a couple of years ago. I really felt that one – he was a good musician and a really nice guy. It was funny to find ourselves in those cellars back among ex-Voltairiens.

But Contagion was going nowhere, just diving into the fog. No gigs on the horizon – what were we practicing for? Something had to be done. Suddenly, I, who had never managed to lift a little finger for my own career, I proclaim myself "manager" of the group. What wouldn't I have done to get some recognition from Freddy?

I started poking around, and the first contract I landed us, which I put under their noses, was a concert in a festival at a pavilion in Paris, at the Porte de Pantin. The biggest Parisian scene of the time. That's where I'd seen Clapton, McCartney and Zappa the week before...

The name of the festival? "Rock Against Police." Promising. It was at the tail end of Giscard's reign, and the freedom-killing laws were multiplying by the minute. The organizer of the festival, an enthusiastic and sympathetic young guy, was having none of it (Rock Against Racism, Rock Against the Prisons…). In general, the protest concerts he organized were a lot of sound and fury. The leftist press complacently relayed the message. When I put the contract in front of them, the members of Contagion celebrated me like a conqueror. We were listed on a beautiful poster next to the headliners, The Inmates, and the best of the French rockers: Océan, Little Bob Story, I forget the others. But we'd really cleaned up: we were going to be the opening act, which turned out to be damned good luck!

The following nights, Freddy, Zouzou and the rest of the band, we all went around pasting the poster up everywhere, especially on top of those of the right-wing Action Française. We hit all the big fences and walls in anticipation of our concert on Sunday. And Sunday, I found myself up on an eighteen meter-wide stage, hooked up to a 15,000 watt sound system, behind my keyboards and before a public of two or three thousand civilians. And the Contagion machine was on a roll. We were playing right up against the speakers, so loud I was stone deaf for the next twenty-four hours. Super reaction from the crowd. So much so, we played two more songs than we'd planned. Then we split, right in time.

Because while we were playing our set, trouble had started backstage. Knowing that he couldn't count on the police to handle any possible unrest, the organizer had called on the security services of two groups. He'd miscalculated. They were two rival gangs, one composed of skinheads, the other a bunch of hairy, studded bikers à la Hell's Angels. Instead of preventing possible disorder, they started a war. While we were on stage, the air was already vibrating with an unhealthy electricity. By the time we got off, we could see what was coming next. Instead of packing up our equipment backstage to stick around and watch the other bands, we decided to decamp to my house in my good old Citroën station wagon. And from there, having dropped off the amps and all our stuff, we went back to the concert.

The battle was in full swing. Smoke was rising everywhere, a whole truck full of beer had been bashed in and robbed. The full cans were being used as ammunition and they were flying overhead. Fistfights, the screams of girls, nunchucks whistling through the air, the first ambulance sirens, the first stretchers... Rock 'n' roll.

The "nice organizer" got on stage to try to calm everybody down when a rowdy kid jumped up and planted a knife in his thigh. The equipment of the group Océan, who'd just played, was reduced to splinters. The Inmates got out just in time... And while all of that was going on, across the way, two or three hundred meters along the esplanade, the paddy wagons of the Republican Security Forces were lined up, and the guards surveyed the scene, smirking, awaiting instructions that never came. "Rock Against Police"? Okay, kids, go for it! Have a ball!

That was Contagion's first concert.

The others were less glorious. A few little clubs, some Youth Culture Centers in the suburbs. I found myself projected back to my high school dream of being in a rock band, but now it had become a sort of nightmare. Lugging all that gear, the keyboards, the drums, the leaden amps, loading all that into our rig just to bust all the shock absorbers, getting lost on the outskirts of nowhere, giving a quickie concert under fluorescent lights in half-empty halls. Retrieve the gear, drink a last, silent beer at three in the morning, and go hit the hay, each one in his own home. All that to earn just enough to pay for the gas used to get to the gig? Was it worth it?

The only thing that could have kept me in this adventure would have been to believe in it. But the truth is that I didn't believe in our repertoire, or in Contagion. And even if I had nothing against Hard Rock, it really wasn't my cup of tea. I dropped out.

I still have some good memories, like that amnesia of a certain night. We had a show in some shithole of a town. I felt pretty bad, my legs were like cotton, my heart beating 140 bpm. While I was having a shot at the bar, I fell off my stool and Cyril caught me just before I would have smashed my face into the floor. Then he took me aside and led me to the green room where we'd left our stuff. He liked to snort smack. He made us two lines and… sniff, sniff! Me, who wasn't used to it, that sent me straight through the roof. And I didn't come down until the end of the show, drenched in sweat and astonished: "It's already over?"

Another time, the inverse scenario. We were straight, but the ambiance was louche. A crowd of drooling semi-thugs, sitting on the ground, bobbing their heads like pigeons. We played our first song, and at the end, a deathly silence. Not a sound, no applause, not even a sniffle, nothing. We tried the second one, and then, after about thirty seconds, general pandemonium in the room. Total desynchronization like that for the rest of the concert. We didn't understand anything. Later, we learned that everybody was tripping on acid.

Ciao then to the gang. Anyway, Contagion imploded a few weeks later – no destination.

A year passed before Freddy reappeared. So long AC/DC – now it was time for The Stray Cats. Strongly impressed by Brian Setzer's amazing musicianship, Freddy had gone rockabilly. He had a pompadour. He was living in a huge apartment behind the Canal Saint-Martin, still with his girlfriend Zouzou, plus a Doberman the size of a calf.

Of course, if he was coming back to me, it was to propose a new association in some crazy scheme. And of course I was willing. Ever the chameleon, I went into the rockabilly thing and whipped off three titles that we recorded, hoping to make a new demo. *"Ni Buick ni Pontiac," "Star ou Fan," "Dancer dans les étoiles"*... His guitar, with all that distortion cleaned away, sounded better than ever. We start believing again. New hopes for our comet. The friendship that still didn't want to say its name starts to ramp up again.

I took him to see Hervé to get his advice about our demo. I always kept Hervé up on what I was doing. But this time, he was unconvinced, and he told me afterwards: "What the hell are you doing with this rockabilly guy? Make your songs the way you know to make them, songs that resemble your paintings!" He always liked my paintings, sort of psychedelic frescos overloaded with miniature figures.

Anyway, Freddy was starting to go off the rails again, seriously, jumping from one mood to another, from bad to murderous. That demo joined the others on the shelf. There are two words that I ended up really hating: "demo" and "project."

Chapter 9
Imre's Bad Trip

One day I received an invitation from the State University of New York in Fredonia to give a lecture on capoeira, the Brazilian martial art. On account of that book that I published on Brazilian dance, the one I recommended to Massahoud, it's a topic on which I'm considered something of an academic authority. My lecture would be during a period in which Imre had planned to be staying with me. I was intrigued by the invitation. It was the name of the place that hooked me. Surely you remember it from that hilarious Marx Brothers film. Aside from my own curiosity, it really seemed like if there were an appropriate place for Imre Lodbrog to play a show, it would be in a fictional republic led by Groucho Marx. But when I checked online, it appeared that the only feasible way to get to Fredonia was by car. I don't drive, but Imre does – in fact, he likes driving, often taking road trips with his kids in his battered old Renault station wagon – and I'm not a bad navigator. I thought I'd scout us out a little venue, and maybe we could hit a few other sights on the way there and back. When I pitched the idea, he immediately said yes.

Of course things are never quite as simple as they seem, and the first glitch was locating a venue. While I'd successfully scored gigs for us in Latvia, Lithuania and Brooklyn by stalking bar proprietors on Facebook,

Fredonia proved a tougher nut to crack. The one club I found on the internet featured mainly wet t-shirt contests. I sent them a little note about our Franco-American lounge act, but unsurprisingly, I didn't hear back. I figured I'd sort that out later. Imre would bring his guitar just in case.

The second glitch had to do with Imre's driving habits. He's used to a stick, but when we went to JFK to pick up our vehicle, they gave us an enormous silver Chrysler van with an automatic transmission. Well, he was willing to give it a go. Before handing us the keys, the clerk walked around the van, ticking off on her form any preexisting scrapes. When I saw there were a couple, I asked her about liability for that kind of thing, and she said in a very reassuring way, "Oh, you're paying for insurance. If you bring it back with another scratch or two, of course it's covered!"

It took us a few minutes to get out of the parking garage. First we couldn't figure out how to adjust the seats, and then there was the unfamiliar transmission. Also, the brakes were very responsive. This combination of factors meant we were kind of heaving and jerking back and forth for a while as the garage attendants looked on in mild dismay.

Now is the moment at which I need to tell you something about Imre's psychic state on this trip. It's true he's prone to some anxiety, but he usually manages to keep it in check through a variety of techniques, including magical thinking, drinking whiskey, noodling on the guitar, and smoking marijuana. There was one other chemical aid he'd been using for some time – a mild serotonin reuptake inhibitor that I'd never heard of. It seems it's more often prescribed for humans in France than in the US. In my country, it's more typically recommended by veterinarians as an appetite stimulant for sad cats. My Internet research revealed that his dosage was exactly twice what's usually prescribed for a thirteen pound cat – a pretty minor intervention even by French standards. I didn't find that particularly worrisome, but Imre didn't like feeling dependant, and this was the moment he'd decided to try to wean himself from it. We both knew there might be a withdrawal issue. I wanted to be supportive, but I suggested he bring along at least a little stash just in case cold turkey proved too difficult.

When we hit the road, he'd been clean for a few days, and nothing too alarming had happened. But as we lurched back and forth in that parking garage, his pupils were pretty dilated, and I thought his breathing seemed a little accelerated. We'd opted to pick the car up at the airport on account of the lower rental prices there, but if you've ever driven into or out of JFK, you perhaps realize how hellish it can be. As soon as we got off the ramp onto the highway, we found ourselves surrounded by 18-wheelers honking manically. Imre was still trying to get the hang of that automatic transmission, so as we filed into line for the toll booth, we were still doing that kind of lurch-and-brake thing. We saw the enormous truck behind us slowly advancing, apparently anxious to get through. I don't remember if the driver was honking – there was so much general cacophony – but we certainly had a sense of somebody's impatience, which was suddenly compounded by the sickening thunk of impact. The guy had hit us, and pretty hard. He was so high up in the cab of the truck, we couldn't make out his face to see if he was looking apologetic or gleeful. But we had the impression it might be the latter. We remembered that early Spielberg movie, "Duel," which depicted a similar scenario, with terrifying results. For Imre, this situation also resonated with that catastrophic road trip to Mexico in '72.

We were in the middle lane of a massive highway filled with other possibly sociopathic monster truckers. We weren't sure if the guy had damaged our van, but it didn't seem like the best idea to lurch through two or three other lanes to get to the shoulder to check it out. I remembered the assurances of that clerk and told Imre to plow ahead for now.

Things thinned out a little past the toll, but suddenly the motor shut off, and the fuel meter plummeted to zero. Fortunately, by this time Imre had maneuvered his way to the far right lane, so we were able to coast off the highway and into the parking lot of a diner. We checked out the rear bumper, which indeed had an ugly gash from our run-in. I rifled through the rental papers and located the emergency number for "roadside assistance."

After some confusing telephone conversations, a guy arrived with a modest little Hyundai replacement vehicle. Back on the road, twilight fast approaching, I spread out before me the print-outs I'd prepared of the Google Maps driving directions. We were taking I-80 through Danville, Bellefonte, and finally Allegheny National Forest. It didn't look too complicated. But of course we should have known better – and I should have insisted on paying the extra fee for GPS. We ended up, to quote Dante, *nel mezzo del cammin di nostra vita*, deep in a pitch-black forest, having taken a guess at an unmarked fork. There were no signs, no lights, and no houses in sight. We had no idea if we were going in the right direction. Just as we were considering turning back, Imre spotted a tiny, flickering light in the distance. We pulled up and saw it was a shack, with a small neon Budweiser sign in the window – a bar! There was a sign posted on the door that said: "WARNING: THIS IS A SMOKING ESTABLISHMENT. ENTER AT YOUR OWN RISK." We looked at each other and pushed the door open.

It was like Snow White stumbling onto the cottage of the seven dwarves. And indeed, there were about seven weird little hippies in there, bearded, disheveled, and drunk as skunks! As promised, they were smoking up a storm. The floor was covered in sawdust. They looked at us with what for a second seemed like malice, but then it became apparent they were just having a hard time focusing through the smoke and whiskey haze. We apologized for barging in and then spread out the Google Maps on the bar and asked if they could perhaps indicate the way out of the woods. The print-outs seemed to flummox them. They kept turning them upside down and sideways, and squinting. The bartender told us to go back the way we came, but the drunkest skunk of all, who barely managed to keep his eyes open, insisted that we'd been on the right path. Something about his certitude inspired more confidence. As we left them there in the smoke and sawdust, the bartender shouted, "Watch out for the bear!" I laughed, but he didn't. He said, "I'm serious."

We decided to forge ahead according to Sleepy's advice – which turned out to be good. In twenty minutes we'd cleared the forest, and soon we were on the outskirts of Fredonia. Civilzation! Sort of. It was nearly midnight when we checked in. The only place to get food was the gas station down the street. Imre wanted to go alone – he could use a little walk after all that driving. He returned fifteen minutes later with a tall boy and a can of barbecue Pringles. We shared them. To tell the truth, they tasted pretty good. I insisted on putting Imre in the tub after that harrowing drive. I stuck my entire forearm in the water to check the temperature, which seemed fine to me, but Imre claimed it was scalding hot and he howled like a wounded beast. Finally, I dried him off, gave him a little back rub, and we both passed out. That's not our typical bedtime routine, but it's a pretty good indication of just how exhausted we were.

That doesn't mean we slept well. Imre had horrible nightmares, and his tossing and turning kept waking me up. In the morning we were both fried. I toddled off to my lecture, while Imre took a walk around the town, such as it was. When I got back back, he seemed subdued. Later he told me that when he'd walked the five or six blocks to the edge of the village, he'd found himself standing, mesmerized, in front of an enormous billboard advertising the Chautauqua County Crisis Hotline.

I could tell Imre was struggling, but my own impulse was just to keep him distracted. In all that Fredonia Googling, I'd stumbled upon some references to Lily Dale, a nearby 135-year-old Spiritualist enclave inhabited entirely by esoteric specialists. That sounded like an interesting side-trip! I'd reserved us a room at a guesthouse there.

As we approached the gates of Lily Dale, we saw a lot of American flags outside the clapboard houses. There were a few people sitting out on their porches, and they seemed to be eyeing us with curiosity, though I guess the same could be said of us eyeing them. Weirdly, once we pulled into the enclave proper, we didn't see any people at all. The houses were modest, though painted some interesting candy colors. There were lawn tchotchkes depicting fairies, elves and trolls in front of many of the residences, and signs in nearly every window saying "So-and-so, Registered Medium," with a phone number. We located our guesthouse, and entered the screened porch, where we found some cozy wicker furniture, plants, more tchotchkes, and a dry erase board showing a list of the rooms with their intended occupants. "Room #8: Barbara B and Imre Lodbrog." All of the other rooms were booked as well, which was odd, because there didn't seem to be a soul around. At the top of the board it said, "Leave your shoes and your worries here on the porch!" At the bottom it said, "Slip your payment under the dragonfly!" I located a small, sparkly painting of an insect with a little slot underneath, and I pushed a check in there.

Imre was nervously flipping through some flyers for workshops and consultations that were neatly stacked in a corner. I suggested we drop our things off in our room. We had, as instructed, removed our shoes.

We padded up the carpeted steps, past some slightly creepy Victorian paintings, and we found room #8. It contained a squeaky old cast-iron bed, lacy curtains, an antique dresser, and more angel and fairy knickknacks. I'd plopped my gear on the bed and was starting to unpack when Imre said, with some urgency, "Bébé, please, let's get out of here." He had a very, very bad feeling. It was those flyers downstairs, offering to put you into contact with your dead dears – including your deceased pets – for a price. Imre was convinced the whole town was occupied by snake-oil salesmen. I thought he was overreacting. Surely some of these people were sincere.

I convinced him to take a walk and think about it. I said if he hadn't changed his mind before sunset then we could find some motel back on the highway. We went downstairs, put our shoes back on, and started wandering through the quiet little rows of houses. We came to the edge of town and saw the sign announcing that we were now entering the pet cemetery.

That's when everything changed. Both Imre and I fell silent. There was a velvety carpet of moss all around, a canopy of dark green leaves, and the dense smell of rotting bark and fungus. We each explored a bit on our own, but would periodically take one another by the hand to see something extraordinary. Finally, pale, Imre said, "Bébé, I was wrong. I want to stay."

If the residents of Lily Dale had been hucksters trying to make a buck off of other people's grief, that would be one thing. But he now understood that they were really, sincerely a bunch of crazy people who couldn't let go of their dead and loved animals like they were family. Imre also can't let go of his dead and he loves animals like they were family. I love Imre.

We held hands and walked back to the guesthouse. We never saw the proprietor or the other guests, though we heard a couple of faint creaking sounds that night of people moving about. For obvious reasons, we didn't want to make that old bed of ours squeak too much. Imre smiled mournfully, noting that this was not exactly the place to "commit sexy follies," but we managed to commune, tenderly, under the watchful eyes of the angel tchotchkes. Medium night of sleep, during which Imre had a very disturbing dream about his father. It was unspoken, but we both knew it had to do with Imre's cold turkey.

Next morning: back on the road again. For the trip back, I'd proposed we take an alternate route, I-86 through Woodstock. I had two very dear friends there, Randy and Jeremy. They own a beautiful home, and I thought we might crash there for a night before returning our rental car. When Imre heard "Woodstock," his face lit up. I thought playing a little house party at Randy and Jeremy's might be fun. But just before we got there, something very sad happened: Jeremy's closest friend, a famous, acerbic comedienne, died unexpectedly during what was supposed to be a minor out-patient surgical procedure. He was devastated, and had to rush back to the city. No house party, needless to say. Randy would be receiving us alone – but he told us warmly that he'd bought a big rack of lamb to cook for us, and he was also baking a lemon tart. Randy is a sweetheart.

We arrived with a bottle of champagne, and Randy showed us the beautiful pool they'd installed in the back. It made a lovely, quiet sloshing sound as we stared up at the starry sky. We sat on the screened deck, with candles all around, and sipped champagne. We could smell the lamb roasting. Randy asked about our trip, and then said, "Well, I have some news for you. You're not going to believe this." He and Jeremy were getting married. It was a sudden decision, though they'd been a couple for many years. It happened at some recent dinner party – they were seated with some legendary civil rights-era judge who said he'd be happy to perform the ceremony if they ever decided to tie the knot, and they looked at each other and thought, "Why the hell not?" Aside from the offer of the legendary judge and the opportunity to throw a great party, it would simplify some legal things about their shared property.

Perhaps you're also encountering this conundrum: a plethora of dear, charming, lovable gay friends who, after years of bemoaning heterosexuals' lemming-like commitment to State-sanctioned contractual monogamy in exchange for questionable economic and legal privileges, are lining up for the same. Perhaps you, too, are simultaneously joyous for their newly acquired civil rights, profoundly moved by their desire to express and share their deep and abiding love for one another, and confused. Randy gets all this – he certainly didn't need me to explain it – but he said the sentimental and pragmatic benefits had finally tipped the scale over their reservations.

Imre also didn't need any explanations regarding the ironies. We'd already discussed the historical origins of legal marriage as chattel slavery. We'd both been legally married early in our amorous careers, and then thought better of things. He'd spent nearly thirty years with the mother of his two daughters without, as the song goes, "putting a ring on it" – not, obviously, out of a fear of commitment, but because neither the State nor any organized religion seemed to him to be in a position to authorize his or anyone else's affective or erotic bonds.

But remember, Imre was in the thick of withdrawal. He was twitchy, sleep-deprived, and, in a phrase, off his gourd. Randy went in to check on the lamb and Imre leapt out of his chair. Trembling, he grasped my shoulders and stared into my eyes. He whispered hoarsely, "Marry me!"

I paused. And then I said, "Imre, no."

I almost never have to say no to Imre. In fact, he once wrote a song for me called "Oui," because I say it so much. But this was out of the question.

We barely managed to compose ourselves before Randy returned, and we struggled to keep up our end of the conversation for the rest of the evening. That was perhaps the most fitful night of the trip, despite the luxurious guest bed and our bellies full of lamb. Imre was inexplicably consumed by jealousy. He was having palpitations. I didn't realize it at the time, but he was also totally plastered. He'd apparently snuck into the kitchen during the course of the dinner to pilfer a few swigs from an open bottle of cooking sherry. Anyway, for whatever reason, as we argued there in bed, nothing I could say seemed to satisfy him. Finally, I started weeping and told him I couldn't take it anymore. We spent the night lying there, twitching, in a barely controlled détente.

We told Randy in the morning that we couldn't dawdle as we had to get the rental car back to JFK. We must have looked a wreck. He insisted we take along a plate of that delicious lemon tart he'd made. We paused in the town center to have one more cup of coffee and talk a little about what was happening. Imre was able to recognize that some of his reactions might be attributable to the chemical adjustment. We both wondered if maybe he shouldn't be taking the weaning thing a bit more slowly.

I worried about Imre having to drive in that condition, but he said he'd be okay. Still, when we got close to JFK, things started to get pretty hairy. Imre began hyperventilating again. He seemed to be flashing back to our Spielberg moment with that crazy trucker. He said he needed to pull over for a minute – he needed to catch his breath. I thought maybe his blood sugar was a little low. He sat there, shaking, on a piece of railing off the shoulder of the road and I fed him some of that lemon tart from my fingers. Eventually, he collected himself and we putt-putted our way back into the rental car garage.

When we got back to my house and unloaded our gear, we realized Imre hadn't once opened his guitar case. That night, he crashed into a deep sleep, in which an enormous grey wolf appeared to him, moaning softly as it emerged from a forest. Maybe you think that was on account of the pet cemetery, but he intuited it had something to do with his ancient dog Ragnar, back in Normandy. Ragnar wasn't well when he'd left, and Imre knew the end was coming soon. Indeed, shortly after awakening, he received a text from his younger daughter, Anouk. Sadly, she told him that Ragnar had left this world.

Poor, gentle Imre. He'd lost another fellow beast.

He did decide to go back on a modest dose of his drug, for a while anyway. After a few days it kicked in and things returned to normal. He may get off it eventually, but he's in no hurry for now. As he later wrote in the song that chronicled our adventures: "If you want to have a nice, peaceful honeymoon, don't forget to bring a needle and a spoon."

You know, rock 'n' roll and drugs have always gone together. It's not necessarily about a voracious desire for more sensation — sometimes it's about needing to feel just a little less.

Chapter 10
The Eclipse

FIVE YEARS FLEW BY without any news from one side or the other. Until the day in '85 when Freddy gave me another sign of life. We saw each other again. He'd changed again, but this time it was more than just a change of look. On edge, cutting, semi-delirious. His character traits were turning caricaturesque, and Zouzou spent much of the time rolling her eyes. I was waiting to hear his next hair-brained proposition, but this time, I wasn't hitching my hopes on his comet. What's more, he didn't seem to really understand who I was. He greeted me, *"Salut François!,"* which I at first decided not to comment on, in the name of our old code of humor. But after he persisted in calling me François a few times, I finally asked him for clarification. "If you want to know," he answered, "go take a stroll around the Château de Meung sur Loire…"

Later, I'd find myself about a dozen times passing just a few kilometers from the Château de Meung without ever making the detour to go in. All I learned was that this château had once sheltered Villon, and that there was a portrait inside of the "damned poet" which, according to Freddy, was my spitting image.

At the time, I was living with my new companion, Atika. I'd fallen head over heals in love with her, to the point of leaving my family moorings. Atika's and my place was also just a few steps from the Canal Saint-Martin. So we were neighbors. But when I invited Freddy one day to visit us at our place for a change, he retorted, "A threshold, one doesn't just cross like that…" What did he mean by that?

His spite at not having made it through music – Freddy had tried to compensate for that through body building. His guitar was stuck in a corner and he wouldn't touch it. The Doberman spent his time stretched out like a rug on the floor. Zouzou had the patience of an angel, but the tips of her wings were starting to moult. I could see things were going downhill. I don't remember anymore exactly how that episode ended, but as time passed, I began to think it had been our last meeting.

As for me, it was a time of change. Claude Massot, the director on that tour of the "rising stars of French song," with whom I've since nurtured a solid friendship, pulls the most unexpected proposition out of his hat. To be his assistant director for the shooting of a documentary in Africa on the traces of a precolonial explorer.

"But I don't know anything about that!"

"If I ask you to do it, it's because I know you're capable!"

Three months in Africa, paid royally, was I going to refuse that? I jumped at the chance!

The completely crazy adventure that ensued has no place in this story. But it took my life in a radically new direction: it was an opening to the world of image – television first, then cinema. Because a few weeks later, while we were driving around the bush in a Land Rover, Claude included me in yet another idea...

Claude was an excellent documentarist, and widely respected in the business. But he was suddenly bitten by that virus that attacks a lot of documentarists: he wanted to move into the realm of fiction, what he liked to call "entering the grown-ups' room." He had this genius idea: to make a fictional film based on the shooting of *Nanook of the North* by Robert Flaherty, reputed to be the first documentary filmmaker. My friend proposed that I join him as his co-scriptwriter.

I'd also never done that. But again, how and why would I refuse?

Those nights under the mosquito nets, lulled to sleep by the laughter of the hyenas and the groans of the hippopotami, we dreamed out loud, and Claude promised our next meeting would be at the foot of icebergs. As soon as we got back from Africa in '84, Claude and I started writing what we were then calling "The Great North." A production house attached itself to the project and sent us to the Poste-de-la-Baleine, in Nunavik, Quebec.

The arctic fascinated me, just as the desert had fascinated me. Between '87 and '93, we made about a dozen trips there, from the Belcher Islands to the Terre de Baffin.

I fed myself with readings from explorers, ethnologists and missionaries. I loved the -50°C, the raw seal meat, devoured right there on the ice, I loved the mystery of the Inuit people, their shamanistic culture and their literally superhuman, millenary endurance.

In those days without end and that landscape without a horizon – the sky and the ice fields blur into one another – I took off on long solitary walks, the headphones of my Walkman on my ears. On returning to France, when I looked at the moon, I half-believed I'd returned from there.

The script we wrote, *Kabloonak,* won the Grand Prize for the Best Screenplay that year. There was an enormous *fiesta* at the chic Closerie des Lilas with all the hotshots from French cinema. We walked out of there stunned, holding in our four arms the heavy trophy with a gold-leafed reel and feather on a marble base. On the financial end, I had no more worries. The production house paid us generously, some other prizes tumbled in, and I was simultaneously working on a few television shows.

And my songs? I got back to work on them. When I went to see Hervé for our customary exchange of creative work, things had really shifted for him in the few years we'd been apart. A cataclysm. He'd put out a third album. Some really good tracks, he thought, except for one, a little song he'd added at the last moment just to finish the thing off. He stuck it at the end of the B-side.

The title of the song? *"Il est libre Max."* The radio stations grabbed it, and soon Max was on the airwaves at a rate of a hundred plays per day. It's not just the radio, it's TV, magazine covers... What one would call today an enormous *buzz*, except not with the ephemerality that the term implies, because *"Il est libre Max"* became one of the eternal classics of French song, practically part of the national patrimony. That little song has been covered millions of times by tons of artists, in creole style, disco, reggae, hard rock... Ask anybody. My kids learned it in school. It's a beautiful song and a beautiful story that shows that you just can't plan success.

Did I envy Hervé back then? Sure, but above all I was happy for him, remembering our conversation at the back of the bus in '74: "Me, I have to succeed at this, because I don't know how to do anything else."

Me, I was still floating like a butterfly. Between my new activities, I threw together a group. A remarkable pair of brothers on bass and drums, plus an excellent saxophonist. We recorded a few numbers in a studio, and I created a little ad hoc look for the lead single, *"L'étrangleur." Succès d'estime.* Somebody told me I was the new Gainsbourg. Thanks a lot. I just wanted to be the next me. One more ephemeral group, an *histoire sensuelle sans suite,* as Gainsbourg himself would have said. A sensual story with no follow-up. What's more sensual than music, besides love?

Then I passed from The Strangler to a kind of hat-bedecked crooner through the weird operation of a new composition, "Loving Room." I recorded it in a studio with some ace session musicians, I painted a story board in gouache, Claude took over the direction, and all that became a video clip that screened on a supposedly sulfurous TV show of the epoch called "Sexy Follies." In the clip, I appear entangled in the arms and sheets of a beautiful naked woman over some colorful paint-box backdrops (the prehistoric ancestor of After Effects).

Finally, after about a dozen return trips to the Canadian arctic, *Kabloonak* was filmed – in Siberia, in '92. Four delirous months on board an ice breaker in the Bering Strait. And as soon as we got back, Claude came up with another crazy idea, for me to compose the music for the film.

That's another story. As for equipment, I'd already given up on my old Revox. The '80s, that was the dawn of the Midi system. So I got myself one, and suddenly there I was behind the control board of an Atari 1040, equipped with Notator. The illusion of limitless horizons. Musically, Midi fucked up a lot of songwriters, among them Hervé. Because basically, it meant giving up on the guitar, the direct source. All those samples were at our disposal, with an infinity of possibilities. At night, we'd go to bed with our eyes red from staring at the screen all day, our heads pounding from having tapped into all that information and all those virtual sounds in a perfectionist delirium, resulting in a kind of aseptic sound emptied out of all feeling. The tragic error had been not to realize that given the galloping pace at which that technology was evolving, the sounds of one day would seem ridiculously obsolete the next. While a guitar and a drumset will always be a guitar and a drumset.

Freddy wasn't fooled by any of that. When I'd see him years later, because I would see him, he would pronounce categorically and without counter-argument: "The '80s, that was the death of music." And for him, "Midi" would only ever mean the boundary between the morning and the afternoon, *le matin et l'après-midi*.

Still, thanks to that technology, I had the pleasure of composing a number of pieces using all the possibilities of those machines. Some crazy 54-track oddities, including "The Gnomes," something along the lines of "Peter and the Wolf," a sonic illustration to a story that I used to tell my son Martin every night.

Martin was born in '83, shortly after my return from Africa. Well, at least nine months after...

You can say what you like about the Midi system, but I must acknowledge that without all that rigmarole, it would have been inconceivable for me to envisage the score for a film on a big screen in Dolby stereo. I spent almost a year tethered to the Atari, elaborating on what the arctic and the story of Nanook had inspired in me. Theme after theme. I used dissonant chords, brass, percussion to give a symphonic dimension to the whole, all of which seemed necessary in order to evoke that lunar country that I'd loved so. I still wasn't sure of anything, but all the same it was an exultant adventure. As there was obviously no question of using those homemade sounds, and since I'd done all that work in the spirit of a... demo, the adventure in question had to be taken up a notch.

October '93, I'm flying to Moscow where the philharmonic orchestra of Mosfilm awaits me in an auditorium the size of a stadium. Seventy musicians are there, waiting for a signal from the maestro. By the fourth tap of the baton, I feel myself lifted off the earth. The main theme invades the space with all its brass, its chords and percussion, altogether real this time. It's like an ocean washing over me! The immense power of an orchestra, which has suddenly transfigured all my solitary labor during those long months in a laughable home studio.

But during the two weeks of recording, Moscow is imploding. It's what will later go by the name of Red October. The revolutionary flags are taken back out of the cupboards, the people take to the streets, television stations are shut down, the army moves in with rocket launchers. A state of emergency is declared. Snipers are positioned on all the rooftops and they fire on anything that moves. The deputies, having lost their chance at a putsch, are locked up in the Duma fortress. Yeltsin sends in the tanks. Duma goes up in flames. They say there are more than two thousand dead. It's hard to make these estimates in Russia... I think of Freddy,

159

who surely would have established some connection between my presence in Moscow and the events that were unfolding there.

At the beginning of '95, *Kabloonak* came out in the theaters. It's a bust. Claude threw himself out the window. He surely had, or thought he had, some other reasons for his despair. But it's true that for him, that bet was all or nothing. Today, there's more praise for the film than criticism, and the praise seems to come from all corners. So this is "posthumous recognition?"

I'd lost another brother. And it looked like the doors of cinema had been slammed in my face. So I find myself back at square one, and I put myself back to work writing songs.

I hadn't forgotten Freddy, and I was worried about him. One day, I ran into Zouzou by chance on the Boulevard Voltaire. She'd finally ended up leaving him, but I had the pleasure of learning from her that he'd had a child with a new companion. A daughter.

And I was naïve enough to believe that that was enough to save him.

Chapter 11
The Normandy Sessions

AFTER THE MILDLY CATASTROPHIC "Bad Trip" through Woodstock, Imre and I decided that our next excursion should be something more relaxing, and closer to his home turf. After all, we'd spent a lot of time on or near mine, in addition to that very disorienting tour of Latvia and Lithuania. And while we'd been together in "Paname," as he likes to call the capital, I had yet to see his actual home. As you know, though he was born in Paris, Imre's primary residence is now a ramshackle cottage in Normandy on a little plot of wooded land. It's near a crumbling cabin where his parents used to take him as a child. He moved to Normandy with Atika about fifteen years ago, between the births of his two daughters. Eventually, Atika and the girls moved out to an apartment in the neighboring town. The girls still come and stay with him sometimes, but he's often there alone, if you can say "alone" about a place so teeming with flora and fauna. There are some trees that he planted there from tiny saplings that are now enormous. He has a small menagerie, including a ferret, rabbits, dogs, a tortoise, cats, and a variety of salamanders and birds. The plants have also proliferated. Imre doesn't like an overly manicured lawn. When he travels, a neighbor comes by to feed the creatures. The flora are on their own.

Imre seemed a little timid about having me stay at his place. I'm not exactly that Eva Gabor character from *Green Acres*, but it's true that my own natural habitat is on the urban end of the spectrum. He wondered how I'd take to his shack. But his dear friend and collaborator, the filmmaker Sandrine Veysset, offered us the beautiful country house that she shares with Ketal Guenin and their son, Sandro. It was a short drive from Imre's, in Conches-en-Ouche. Sandrine and her family were going to be traveling. They asked if we could feed their chickens and cats, and said we'd be welcome to use the music studio in the attic. Ketal, like Sandrine, works in the film industry, but he's a great music enthusiast and he plays the electric guitar. Ketal had also generously offered Imre access to his cellar full of snails.

Imre seemed excited to be able to put me up in such palatial digs. Of course, I immediately wondered if I could get us a gig in the area. The Internet provided exactly zero information on live music venues in Conches-en-Ouches, but Ketal said that in fact there was one little restaurant in town with a terrace, and on occasion somebody played there. I was pretty sure we could worm our way in.

When we got there, I saw the house was just as beautiful as I'd been told. Sandrine and Ketal's place is just around the corner from the town proper, behind a fence and down a sloping drive. It's very private. And though it's large, it feels very cozy, filled with Sandrine's own Matisse-like paintings, colored glass, flea-market furniture, and Ketal's record collection. It's the kind of house that makes you feel immediately at ease. They'd given us our choice of rooms, but Imre thought the coziest was Sandro's, which had colorful walls that he'd scribbled on, and some shelves stocked with model planes and board games. We gave the bed a test run. It did very nicely. After the test run, Imre jammed a little, naked, on the electric guitar. He seemed very relaxed.

That week was heaven. Well, there was one small glitch, which I'll get to in a minute, but for the most part, we spent our mornings writing in bed and our afternoons canoodling in the sunshine. We had a lot of picnics involving wine and charcuterie. Imre insisted I should try *andouille*, a local specialty. It's a kind of cured meat with a very lacy, intricate pattern. That sounds delicate, until you figure out that it's made of compressed pig intestines. It took me a while to understand that myself. When I asked Imre what it was made of, he said that his father's response to such queries about food was always, *"C'est plein de bonnes choses."* It's full of good things. He also made me try *andouillette*, a related sausage. As Wikipedia later informed me: "True *andouillette* is rarely seen outside France and has a strong, distinctive odor related to its intestinal origins and components." The good news is that we ate it with some delicious purple beans that were growing in the garden.

The kitchen was very rustic, with colored tiles on everything, and there was an open birdcage in the window, home to a semi-domesticated dove named Josephine, who came and went at her leisure. The cats turned out to be a rag-tag clowder spawned by a brownish-black queen with a club-foot and one scarred, gaping eye. In fact, her offspring all had eye troubles, apparently suffering from conjunctivitis, which we hoped was just a brief and passing affliction.

In the evenings we'd watch old films. Sandrine has an extensive collection of DVDs, and there were all kinds of books of cinematic history and criticism. There were a few films Imre was anxious to show me, including one he'd written for Sandrine about fifteen years ago. It was an understated but devastating story of a young woman who's come unhinged. Imre's daughter Lucie had played this woman's daughter. Her performance was quiet, riveting, and utterly natural.

Imre also wanted to show me some old favorite films of his, like the comical *"La fiancée du pirate,"* by Nelly Kaplan. It was made in 1969, and it's about an ethical slut with great business sense living in the French boondocks. Imre often turns me on to women filmmakers, and though he doesn't arrange this on purpose, they're his most frequent collaborators. I don't think he wanted to turn me on to *"La fiancée du pirate"* because Nelly Kaplan was a woman, or even because I might vaguely resemble the central character in my history of polymorpous perversity. I think he just thought it was a remarkable film. It was.

We made a couple of day trips. Imre took me to the Moulin d'Andé, an artist's colony where he sometimes goes to work. The Moulin became famous when Truffaut decided to film there. Parts of *Jules and Jim* were shot on the grounds, as well as *The 400 Blows*. It's the Seine that flows through the Moulin, though of course the river has an entirely different character there than it does in Paris. It's so bucolic. There's a small island in the middle inhabited by two old goats. I lay down by the bank of the river and listened to the birds and smelled the grass, and in seconds I was out cold. Imre waited patiently for me to wake up. While he watched me, he made up a song he called *"La Sieste au Bord de l'Eau,"* a nap by the waterside.

Later, Imre took me all the way to the coast, though I didn't fall asleep there. Oh, but before I get to that, I should really tell you about the glitch that I mentioned. About our gig that didn't happen. Well, obviously, we were feeling pretty lazy and relaxed in Conches-en-Ouche, so I hadn't even bothered to worry much about getting a booking at that restaurant that Ketal had mentioned. I figured we just had to walk in and announce ourselves as musicians and they'd welcome us with open arms. So after a few days of picnicking, napping, and, as the song goes, strummin' on the ol' banjo, Imre and I finally trekked up the hill into town, which is basically one street lined with picturesque 15th-century half-timbered buildings. The ground floors are mostly occupied by small businesses – bakeries, knickknack shops, barbers, and a real estate agency. We paused in front of that one. There were several pictures of little bungalows in the area, some of which seemed unexpectedly affordable. We both stared at the pictures, and obviously, we were fantasizing about having one of those for ourselves. I think I was the one who broke the silence. I said, "Imre, let's buy a house in the country."

That surprised even me – not just because of the impracticality (neither of us is what you'd call a "person of means") – but also because of that *Green Acres* discrepancy I mentioned before. Due to his sensitivity, his attachment to animals, and his need for cyclical patterns to appease his anxieties about the passage of time, Imre not only likes but needs to spend a lot of time in nature – but I'm quite the city slicker. Still, there was obviously something about Normandy that was getting under my skin. He seemed to be deeply moved by the idea.

Later, when he reported all this to Sandrine, she tried to reconcile my bucolic and domestic enthusiasms with everything Imre had told her about my fierce independence and urbanity. She said, *"Comment, tu l'as tournée comme une crêpe?!"* The phrase "you flipped me like a pancake" became something of a running joke between us.

So after the little reverie in front of the real estate agency, we continued traipsing up the hill, happy like that, holding hands and fantasizing about a common country life, when we suddenly found ourselves in front of the restaurant in question – an inviting little bistro called the "Braderie Gourmande," which called itself not merely a "restaurant," but also a *"lieu de vie,* lounge, *salon de thé,"* and *"cave à vin,"* with a "panoramic view of the valley." Well, that sounded perfect – until we saw it: the poster on the door, advertising a live performance that weekend by a blues duo going under the artistic moniker "Lil' Red and the Rooster."

DOPPELGÄNGERS. The spitting image of Imre Lodbrog et sa Petite Amie. Dead ringers. As the kids say: wtf? Once we'd registered this blow, we rethought the cold call to the management. We decided to stroll around a bit more to regroup. Suddenly, we began to notice the Lil' Red publicity notice in the window of nearly every business establishment on the main drag. It was really weird. They'd practically wallpapered Conches-en-Ouche with the thing. We even retraced our steps to that real estate office and found it tucked in with some ads for yoga classes and a Neolithic art exhibit.

Imre didn't seem particularly put out by this. If Lil' Red and her purple Rooster had beat us to the punch, he was happy enough to cede the gig to the competition. But being slightly more tactical about such things, I insisted on doing some Internet reconnaissance when we got back to the house. It turns out Lil' Red is a nice red-blooded American gal with Midwestern roots and what would appear, from photographic evidence, to be a taste for partying, while her sidekick, "Pascal," is a native Normandy bluesman and a devotee of T-Bone Walker and Tiny Grimes.

Don't laugh. Imre has a massive hard-on for Mississippi John Hurt.

Well, go figure how that corn-fed Lil' Red ended up with her Norman bluesman in Bernay, France. I did mention, didn't I, that I'm from Wisconsin? It was clear we'd been scooped. We threw in the towel and went to their show. There were some toe-tapping, white-haired patrons scattered around the terrace enjoying, as we were, a glass of white wine. The view, as promised, was panoramic. And the band was entirely plausible. They had a pretty vast repertoire, mostly covers but a few jaunty originals as well. Lil' Red had pluck, all right, and her rooster was brooding but supportive. Halfway through the show a very attractive couple arrived, both in motorized wheelchairs. He was wearing a leather jacket and she had on heavy eye make-up. They were greeted warmly by the wait staff – evidently they were regulars – and space was made for them in an area with good lines of sight. They both lit up cigarettes and fondled each other throughout the show. It was very sexy, and I felt it gave me license to fondle Imre.

So, oh well, no gig in Conches – but we spent quite a few happy hours going over our own repertoire in the attic studio, and also in a cozy corner of Sandrine and Ketal's dining room. We recorded our practice sets and called them the Normandy Sessions. Actually, we called them the Legendary Normandy Sessions. And when you look at the footage we shot of our practice sessions, indeed, I think we look pretty legendary. Somehow in Normandy it didn't matter if Imre was a legend in his own time, or just in our own minds.

At the end of the week, Sandrine and Ketal and Sandro came home, and we shared a meal of Ketal's famous escargots and some ceviche I'd prepared with Imre. We thanked them profusely and packed our gear into Imre's clunker. It was the moment of truth: we'd decided to spend the last few days at Imre's ramshackle hut. At this point, I was so stoned on nature I felt like I could take anything. Of course, it wasn't nearly as derelict as he'd led me to believe. It was small and rustic, but thoroughly charming. He'd cleaned up a bit in anticipation of my visit – particularly the outhouse-like structure he calls his *"capharnaüm"* – a little studio where he writes and records most of his music. He'd actually taken a photo of it before the cleanup, conceding it was something of a natural disaster that deserved documentation.

But even in its confused state, it had a Lodbroggish logic to it. The miscellany of modern and outmoded equipment, magical talismans, photos of himself and his kids, and, above all, a cockamamie assortment of musical instruments made the perfect little protective lair for the production of what, over the last fifteen years, had surely surpassed a couple of thousand songs. He'd thrown these on the heap of all the thousands that had come before, words and chords scribbled into notebook after coffee-soaked notebook.

He shared some of those with me, along with a yellowed newspaper clipping from 1974 announcing his performance at a *"dîner-spectacle."* At the age of 22, the writer claimed, he had "a repertoire of 350 songs. On the stage," the author continued, "one would believe him to be in transit. Barely there, one senses he's already elsewhere, in a rush to escape the very public that both attracts and disturbs him." His photo in the article appeared to illustrate this elusive quality.

When he was cleaning up the *capharnaüm*, Imre had unearthed some other remarkable things that he also showed me, at night, outside, under a flickering light: two wonderful scrapbooks he'd assembled from adventures he'd concocted with each of his sons, and two volumes of poetry by that young pianist he'd known in his early twenties, when he was studying at the *École Normale de Musique*. They'd had an intense but unconsummated romantic friendship, and after he'd left Paris, she took her own life, leaving him a letter absolving him of any responsibility but expressing her passion. Her mother had delivered this letter to Imre with tenderness and without a drop of blame. Still, the story haunted him. Over the years, he's lost several people this way. It seems he's drawn to very sensitive creatures, or perhaps they're drawn to him.

Marie-Isabelle's poems were startling. They were bleak, but quick-witted, with some of the same insistent rhyme schemes and wordplay that mark Imre's songwriting. Occasionally I thought I might have caught an oblique reference to him – a street name, a green eye.

The scrapbooks were also very touching. Imre told me that one year, lacking funds to take him on a proper trip, Imre had proposed to his older son, Tom, that they spend one week in the woods, with only a few supplies – some water, butane, cooking oil, a bag of lentils – and hunt and forage for their survival. Imre had documented each meal with a fancy description of what they'd prepared (plenty of dandelion salad and ragouts of mushrooms) and photographs of Tom eating – evidently ravenously. There were also a few small birds they'd caught in traps, and, on one occasion, a pheasant.

The trip with Martin, his younger son, involved a week-long hike with a very recalcitrant donkey named Henri Pissenlit. Henri nearly drove them crazy, but they ended up quite attached, and cried at their parting.

The last full day of my stay, Imre drove me up to the coast, to the uncanny cliffs of Varengeville. It's like another planet. The immense, stark cliffs are in a constant, slow state of decomposition: first falling off as boulders, then breaking down into stones, and finally disintegrating into particles of sand. Imre had shown me a passage from a novel he'd written, in which an old man stands on the cliff and contemplates this stony degeneration, the mixed in bones of suicides, of unfortunate drunks who might have come to the edge for a last piss, *"glissés, trébuchés, basculés dans un cri, avalés par le vide, écrabouillés en bas!"* – slipping, stumbling, toppling over with a cry, swallowed by the vacuum, crushed below! The old man surveys the scene (and I quote): "In his noggin, this is the great confusion of space and time." The weird, crumbling seascape seems to him *"le plus lointain des pays,"* the most distant of all countries: his own lost youth. The novel was never published, but Sandrine made the story into a film.

The narrative, in brief, is about the encounter between a young boy and the old man he will become. Needless to say, the child's terror and wonder at the passage of time is also Imre's. From the outset, his life was marked by a debilitating anxiety about the passing of the minutes, hours, days, years. Imre needs the grass, weeds and trees, the cliffs, rocks and sand to make sense of all this. Still, the passing of time sometimes keeps him up at night.

The next morning, he drove me back to the airport for my flight back to New York. We'd had excellent luck with the weather during my stay, but that morning there was a deluge. It was coming down so hard the wipers were entirely useless. We had to pull over for a while, and, as though emulating the raindrops, tears also fell from Imre's eyes. He was sad the Normandy Sessions were ending, and so was I, but he was also feeling that bigger sadness, the one about time passing.

Why am I more placid about that? It's not that I care less. I just don't seem to hear the clock ticking. I mean, I know it is, and of course sometimes I'm struck by how quickly my own five decades have passed, but I have the impression there's still plenty of time left for both of us. I even wrote a lullaby to remind Imre of that when he gets overwrought about time. I did the math and gave him a rough estimate of what I thought was a reasonable accounting: "If you're worried and you can't sleep, close your eyes and just remember: we have twenty-nine years."

Chapter 12
Freddy, the Return

BEYOND THE IRREPARABLE LOSS, Claude's death signaled for me the end of my voyage in the world of cinema. At least that's what I thought then. I always thought of my life as a mosaic and I was always ready for everything, come what may. Regarding that loss, I should say that, as in the case of my father, I have this strange conviction that Claude always follows me with one eye, often rejoicing over my good moments and sympathizing with my bad ones. A true presence in his absence. That's not just a poetic chimera, it's something I feel profoundly.

Like a cat, my life landed once again on its feet. A certain Antoine de Cazotte had participated in that "Loving Room" clip, as production assistant. An unusual guy, open, generous, a former hippie, and slightly cracked. We quickly warmed up to each other.

Returning from Père-Lachaise, where I'd just seen Claude dissipate in smoke floating into the sky, I had no desire at that moment to see anybody, but I went to see Antoine. We had a few drinks, smoked a few joints. We remimisced about that euphoric moment when, under the most furious of blizzards, the *Kiev*, our ice-breaker for the *Kabloonak* shooting, was silhouetted like a gigantic whale trapped in the floes, back-lit by the enormous light projectors that illuminated the scene.

The dogs howled at death. We also howled, but at life.

In the course of that visit, Antoine speaks to me of Solveig, whom he recently met and with whom he's obviously in love. She's looking for someone to write a screenplay. He says he thought of me from the start, that he's already spoken of me as a machine gun of a writer, and that now's the time for us to arrange a meeting. Do I agree to the idea? I listened to all that in a blur, it wasn't the moment for enthusiasm, but for the thousandth time in my life, why would I have said no?

Two days later, I got a call from Solveig, two hours later I was ringing her doorbell. Solveig Dommartin, the angel in *Wings of Desire*. She was obsessed with love and with the idea of making a filmic waltz where a great number of characters and destinies would cross in Paris around a theme that never goes stale: Love. This project was, for her, an almost militant act, as if love were in peril, and it needed to be saved before it was too late. Would I write a script for her? Solveig had a solar quality, her energy, her enthusiasm, her pioneering conviction conquered me, and one more time, with feeling, I say, "I'm in!"

We decided to make a short, which would be the teaser for the full-length film. That was *"Il suffirait d'un pont,"* shot on the Canal Saint-Martin, in front of the famous Hôtel du Nord, with a damned beautiful collection of actresses and actors. It was on that shooting that I met Gregory Hervelin, twenty years my junior, and whom I continue to call my "big little brother" (he's 6'4"), my friend Greg.

Besides that, Solveig confided to me one evening that she dreamed of recording an album and she asked me if I'd like to write some songs for her. She told me that she knew some people in that universe as well. One evening we found ourselves in Montreuil in a little gathering at the home of a couple of friends of hers, with Marianne Faithful. Urbane and really friendly, not pulling any rock star attitude at all, and I had the quite surreal privilege of picking up a guitar and introducing her to the magnificent "Days" by The Kinks. "How did I miss this one?," she wondered.

I wrote about fifteen songs in fifteen days for Solveig. We recorded them. We took them around to a few labels. They liked the songs but they were suspicious of her. She had a reputation all over Paris as an uncontrollable electron, never mincing her words, leaving a smoky trail of scandal wherever she went. And also, they told us "kindly," it wasn't enough to have been Wenders' woman to call yourself a singer. The recordings now sleep in a folder called *"les chansons de Solveig."*

Films, songs, all that sank in troubled waters. Solveig had a problem. Alcohol, which, of course, was just the mask of another problem, deeper, and which will remain a mystery. Solveig died a few years later from a sort of cardiac failure, in a hotel room, alone. On the day of her burial, there was an enormous snow storm. But across all the storms, what remains with me, as it must remain for everyone who knew her, I think, is the image of a sun.

For the second time, the doors of cinema seemed to close for me. In order to bounce back, I threw myself into an absorbing task. After Martin's birth, I'd taken one photo of him each week, month after month, year after year, with the same framing – all this without any precise idea of what I'd do with the material. At the time, in '95, a new technique was arriving in the sphere of image-making: morphing. I told myself that all those almost identical images of the same face "morphed" from one to the next over the course of the years could make for an interesting voyage through time. And to make it even more interesting, I decide to begin with the last image of Martin at the age of sixteen, moving backwards toward the first, that of a newborn still covered in vernix caseosa. I composed a sort of sonic dough to wrap it in. That became "Sic Transit," a little televisual acid trip that ended up being broadcast on Canal +.

But music became, more than ever, my secret territory. And bit by bit, tired of composing and recording songs for nobody and for nothing, I begin to forget about it myself.

I saw my friend Greg every once in a while. Twenty years separate us, but a lot of things draw us toward one another, including a passion for drugs – as users, but not only. Lewis Carroll, Timothy Leary, Albert Hofmann... All that interests us. Gregory and his girlfriend Aurélie form such a united couple that I call them Gregoreli. And twenty years later, now that they have two kids, I call them all Gregorélians. A dynasty.

One day, at the end of '97, Greg attacked me in a conversation: "I want to shoot a short. You want to write it for me?" Of course! He just gave me two stipulations: it had to be about kids, and it had to take place in New York. That suited me. Obviously, I didn't get my hopes up. How did this young up-start imagine he could shoot a film in New York? It looked like totally adolescent delirium (he was twenty-two years old), after a big fat joint...

Eight months later, we were in New York, where Gregoreli were already installed, preparing the terrain. The screenplay was written in a flash. I amused myself by crafting a remake of Snow White and the Seven Dwarves, the latter turning into a little gang of rappers from the Bronx, and Snow White owing her name to her eager consumption of white powder.

By the time I arrive, the only thing left to do is say, "Action!"

A good month of pure pleasure in New York under the sign of Snow White. New York, I'd been there five or six times since '72, but in '98 it really wasn't the crazy city I first met at nineteen. Giuliani had been through town, installing his millions of security cameras all over the place. With the redoubled surveillance and a quadrupled police force, he'd succeeded in transforming what had been the city of crime and danger into a kind of giant theme park for big kids. All the disquieting electricity had dissolved in the air. You could walk around at all hours of the day and night, in the streets, in the subway, without risking your skin. An efficient method that would inspire our own Sarkozy, who liked to talk about sandblasting the *banlieues* of Paris to clear out the riff-raff...

When I got back to Paris, a friend introduced me to Sandrine, who'd directed, among other things, a beautiful film that had done very well, *"Y' aura t-il de la neige à Noël?"* She was looking for a scriptwriter... We immediately took to one another. Since then, we've written three films together.

The year 2000 arrived. Here I send the reader back to my first chapter... The move to the country, a few years of happiness, the birth of Anouk, the death of my father, the beginning of the roller coaster ride…

It's then, in February of 2008, that I receive a phone call from the one high school friend I still have: Olivier Cauquil. He's calling to tell me that Freddy's popped up again, that he contacted him to ask him for my number…

"So do I give it to him?"

"Of course! What a question?!"

"It's just that he seemed to me… bizarre, on the phone."

And since when didn't Freddy seem bizarre? Two weeks later, Freddy calls me. His scratchy voice, caustic but friendly, tells me that he's harnessed to his Revox, the same one we'd recorded my songs on back in my place on the Dead End. And, in sum, he proposes that we get back in the saddle! We agree to meet at Olivier's at the beginning of May. In fact, we end up changing the plan. I speak with Freddy again by phone. He doesn't have enough cash to take the train, from what I can understand. But me, I have my car, and Cherbourg isn't exactly the end of the world for a friendship of nearly forty years. "I'll be there next week," I tell him. When I take the opportunity to ask him what he's been up to, he sends me for a hike: "Enough blah-blah-blah on the phone. I'll be waiting for you."

While Cherbourg may not be the end of the world, it's still the end of France. Five hours' drive from Pourry. We'd agreed to meet on a street corner not far from the station. I was determined to get there on time, since, naturally, Freddy didn't have a cell phone, and never would. On the agreed upon corner at the agreed upon time, I ask myself what Freddy could possibly look like today... When he taps me on the shoulder, from behind.

"What a great face!" I said to myself. The silvery mane, the creased features, a savage air. But there was a detail that struck me – I realized that his gaze was marked by a slight but obvious walleyed skew that I'd never noticed before. Had he had an accident?

We shook hands.

"Where's your car?"

"Over there!"

He guided me to his house, down a narrow street where my Renault Nevada just fit. On the way, I tried again to make a little small talk. And that made him gripe again:

"Aw, no! We're not going to start with the, 'Hey, how ya doin'? And you, how ya doin'?' We're musicians. I've set up everything we need to get back to work. It's over there, on the left. There, park there!"

Everything in the imperative for Freddy. And me, completely docile.

I get to his house. Before making a mental inventory of his unusual digs, how could I not focus on the little reception corner that immediately gave me a lump in the throat?

A live amp, guitar plugged in, a table, two glasses, a bottle of whisky and a supermarket birthday cake with two candles on top. Freddy strikes a match. Each of the candles is shaped like the number "2". Two two. He explains: "It's been twenty-two years since we've seen each other!"

For the first time in forty years, our friendship says its name.

Freddy has always been but a mask of himself. He thought it best to identify his sensitivity as a weakness, and to camouflage it under badass airs, but given his family history, maybe he had no choice. And he'd become a badass for good. But I can tell he's happy. Happy that I'm there, that I'd come all that way by car just to see him again, now that all the old doors of his old friends had been slammed in his face, happy about the music that will reunite us. His ambitions are, again, without limits. But first he has to clarify a certain point about me...

"Just one question, Seb: Are you dead or are you alive?"

I had a little inner seizure. For a second, I didn't know how to respond. Freddy didn't give me the time to get emotional. "Listen, I've heard that you're a screenwriter, that you have a little family life and all of that." (I suppose Olivier had mentioned that.) "Well, good for you, but I don't give a shit. For me, you're a musician, a guy who makes songs, with badass lyrics. So think about it. If you're alive, you'll get back to music, you'll practice your guitar and we'll make a group, the two of us. And we'll get on stage! This time, there's no next time. So?"

"I'm in, Freddy!" I said.

Then, we plugged in our guitars and started to play. And once again, he kicked my ass. I still didn't know what the fuck he'd been doing all these years, but one thing was for sure, he hadn't put away the guitar, and his playing dumbfounded me maybe more than ever. He'd named his guitar Daphné. The name was written on it in silver letter stickers.

In fact, he actually had put away the guitar – for fifteen years. That was the real wonder.

Late at night, without my asking anything, Freddy launched into the story of his eclipse:

"When my mother died, half my brain froze."

So that explained the weird walleyed skew…

"A whore picked me up, I had a kid with her."

"You really shouldn't talk about your kid's mother like that," I said.

"So how do you call a woman who picks up Johns on the streets of Pigalle every night?"

"…"

"I got sixty grand when I sold the apartment on the rue du Chemin Vert, she skinned me for all of it. I ended up pushing shopping carts at the Auchan Supermarket seven hours a week. I shaved my head and I stuck a feather to my skull. In the neighborhood, everybody called me Geronimo. I was gone."

This slog lasts for a while. The times are rough on Freddy, who one day finds himself as much plucked as he is feathered. There's a toothache involved…

"I got a sore tooth but I didn't have any money to take care of it. Then I remembered Ecuvillon. You remember Ecuvillon? He was at Voltaire. He became a dentist. I called him at his old number and his parents told me that he'd opened a dental clinic in Annecy. So I went to Annecy. But Ecuvillon fucked me over, I think he wouldn't even open the door. I'd spent all the money I had for a one-way ticket. He left me in the street – and I stayed there. There I was in the streets of Annecy… For six years. Annecy, that's in the mountains. In the winter, it's twenty below. So, not to die of cold, I walked. When you're in the streets, if you don't want to die, the only thing to do is walk. And from walking, I became an animal. It gave me a claw, look!…"

He takes off his big pink shoe, then his sock, and shows me, in effect, a sort of sixth toe, a horny thing that shouldn't be there. A claw.

"Never mind about the faggots! Since I was a good-looking guy, I had to keep a bicycle chain with me to defend my ass. That one…" A bicycle chain is coiled on the night table.

I listened to all that. I was like a kid mesmerized by his grandfather's stories.

The end of the story? Freddy was in the streets, SDF – *sans domicile fixe,* homeless – but he was still Freddy, he hadn't given anything up, not his dignity, his internal revolt that kept him standing in his boots against the winds and the tides. He hadn't succumbed to alcohol or filth or begging.

He did little odd jobs here and there, he got a little change to pay for his showers in the public baths and clothes washing at the laundromats. And if anything was left over, he'd buy a croissant. A wandering figure in the streets of Annecy.

A figure that didn't escape the attention of a Russian painter who was living in the town. He tapped Freddy and asked him if he'd pose for him, for pay. Freddy deigned to accept. A while later, a very rich eighty-year-old Jewish lady who owns a big mansion in town passes by the painter's gallery, and is struck by the beautiful face represented on the canvass in the window. (Oh how I wish I could see that painting!) The old lady asks who the model is. The painter tells her, "It's a homeless guy who hangs around the neighborhood." A meeting takes place.

After having flipped for Freddy's face, the old lady is deeply touched by the man and his situation. She offers to shelter him at her residence, where she lives alone. He could do some small jobs for her, her shopping and so on... Freddy moves into the old Jewess's mansion, in a room that she designates as his. There's a tiger skin rug spread out on the floor. Just the day before, the man was sleeping in a frozen parking lot, gripping a bicycle chain. Freddy adapts. Except a bed seems to him too soft, and he chooses instead to spend his nights stretched out on the tiger skin rug.

Freddy, who hated emotionalism, couldn't help being visibly moved when he evoked "the old Jewess." And then one day, or rather one night...

"One night I wake up with a start. I feel that something's not right. I get up and sit at the table. And there, listen to what I'm telling you, I empty myself out of myself. Do you understand that, Seb? My whole being was like a fucking open tap. I was in the process of becoming an empty envelope..."

I squirm in my chair.

Freddy continues: "But just then, I saw something come in through the window. It was a shape, it came up to me slipped inside me. And just at the moment when I was supposed to be completely empty, this form filled me..."

Everything starts spinning in this damn crazy room of his. My throat dry, I empty my glass in one gulp.

Freddy finishes me off. He fixes his eyes on mine: "What that means, Seb is... the guy who's speaking to you at this moment... It's not me..."

The dawn rises through the window. I am physically and nervously spent. I have to lie down. I've brought along a camping mattress, I collapse onto it. Freddy, he's not sleepy. I hear him shuffling around in his big pink shoes like an animal in a cage, before grabbing the guitar and playing a few furious riffs. Until finally calm settles on the room and my eyelids shut under a leaden sleep, only to be awakened soon by a sickening smell. Freddy is up grilling us two slices of beef heart for breakfast, sprinkled with the last bit of his cheap whiskey, a real drain opener. And then we attack another twenty-five hour day.

The grilled beef heart, that's Freddy's regular fare. Not expensive and nourishing, he says. It's all he eats. I think to myself that scurvy is just one more thing that he has to worry about. I want to buy some fruit and milk for him, but Freddy gets pissed off. He has a horror of charity. Always his damned dignity, but also, a kind of nobility: I was his guest! Later I'd manage to get these provisions, telling him that they were for me and then forgetting them when I left, certain that they wouldn't last long.

It's when we go shopping together that I really see how nicely our society is set up. On the supermarket shelves, respectable products are displayed at eye level, within easy reach, physically and economically – for some. But when you're broke, you have to get on your knees. The low-class products are at floor level.

While we chew, Freddy takes up his story again. The old lady took care of him like a son. She pulled some strings and got him *smicard* – "wage earner" – status. Now he's got a little monthly income. But soon a spoilsport sticks his big nose in the story. It's the old lady's real son. Well, put yourself in his place. Who is this handsome charlatan who's come to plant himself in the mansion, who's seduced your mother to the point of… Just before a fabulous inheritance should be coming…? The son made a fucking ruckus, and threatened to have Freddy forced out.

Freddy doesn't want any confusion. He takes his bicycle chain and bows out. One morning, he's not there anymore. But he's another man. Annecy, the streets, that hell – that's over. Paris has nothing to offer him anymore. When one comes back to earth, one thinks of one's cradle, that of one's family. Freddy's family was originally from Cherbourg. It's there that he used to pass his childhood vacations, at his grandmother's. Some distant cousins still live there. Freddy finds their trail and gets a one-way ticket to Cherbourg, with three missions in his head: To find a roof, to get back to music, and to prepare to find his daughter again. The whore's daughter, fourteen years old now.

His cousins help him find a roof, a guitar. The roof, it's an unhealthy sub-basement of a bordello in a bad neighborhood. The very place where I was hearing this story. Freddy plugs up the cracks and holes and sets up the interior. It almost feels cozy in there. Indirect light, nice decor – but no running water. As for the decor, though he didn't pay much attention in putting it together, each element carries its own symbolic force. Some scrawled words, some portraits with the heads cut off, some upside-down posters, a child's self-portrait... Freddy explains to me: "That's my daughter. She drew that picture for me. It's the only image I have of her."

Not only has her mother forbidden him all visitation rights, but Freddy is also prohibited from the entire perimeter of their daughter's school and residence. And that holds until she reaches the age of sixteen. There are two more years to wait. That's all Freddy's waiting for. I think of this girl, I think of this father, I think about the day of their meeting. Her name is Daphne.

And then, no time to breathe, he plugs in the guitars (I'd brought mine). And we practice. What is it we're practicing, anyway? My latest songs gleaned from my latest notebooks are not very convincing, my fingers shake on the fretboard, it all feels rusty. Freddy, on the other hand, is a miracle. How, after all these years in the street without touching a guitar, how could his playing be intact? This guy must have played guitar before his birth, and he'll play it long after his death. I love hearing him, seeing him play. I film him, and strangely, he lets me do it. I invent a little bullshit about how we might be able to use the footage...

Freddy sticks it to me. "You have to practice your guitar, and you have to work on these songs so they're worthy of your name! And then... You have to find a name."

"A name?"

"Yes! A name! Sébastien Régnier doesn't mean anything in rock. Plus you're bald! Me, now, I'm Croogger! Freddy Croogger! With two Gs!"

From time to time during my stay, for no apparent reason, I start to suffocate. I need air. Then I force the beast out of his den and we take a walk around Cherbourg. Freddy shows me the places where he used to play when he was a kid. We go all the way to the port to look into the giant pit where the legendary submarine "Le Redoutable" is docked. Freddy has his habitual itineraries, like the fox has his haunts. As he walks, his eyes scan the scene. When he spots the silhouette of a homeless guy in the distance, Freddy crosses the street. When he sees a sack of old clothes, his gaze narrows, and then he turns away. He'd like to forget his years in the streets, but all of the reflexes of a cagey animal, on the defensive, are still there. These walks are varnished with somber reflections, half-whispered, like: "The world is two times overpopulated. The thing to do would be to go out with a shotgun and shoot one guy out of two."

And then there's the touching detail that he tells me. Not long ago, Freddy was hanging out at a Fnac – the French retail chain – just to keep himself up on what was selling in the world of music. In the rock 'n' roll section, on a book rack, he spots a new biography of Téléphone, and he starts to flip through it… One passage grabs him by the neck: "In tracing the origins of the group, one finds a formation that dates back to high school days: Semolina, composed of Daniel Roux on bass, Richard Kolinka on drums and Frédérique Tchékovitch on guitar…" This belated and relatively anecdotal recognition felt to Freddy like justice finally rendered. That retroactively brightened the whole of his life; it was obvious as I heard him tell the story. My emotions were running higher than they would have been twenty years before – when he probably would have taken the short citation badly, and reacted with his customary aggressivity. Now that it struck him as long-awaited glory just confirmed how far he'd fallen in the interval.

Exhausted, barely standing, both sad and relieved, I tear myself away from Cherbourg. And on the road home, it pops into my head: Imre Lodbrog! That's my new name.

A few weeks later, a second trip to Cherbourg. He's taken over finding a name for our "group." Richelieu Duo. In the '60s and '70s, there was a Parisian club that will always be remembered, as will its founder, Henri Leproux: Le Golf Drouot. In addition to offering relatively inexpensive concerts with the best international rock of the period (The Who, The Stones…) as well as our own national glories (Johnny, Sylvie, les Variations, Eddie & Co….), Leproux had the idea of organizing every Friday evening his famous springboard for fledgling groups and artists. The audience, the only jury, would determine the winner, who would benefit from record sales, concert bookings, etc. A nice little promotional operation for both sides. Me, I'd often been among the feverish spectators, but Freddy had actually gotten up on the legendary stage. I think he even won one of those contests. Anyway, the place had helped to spread his reputation as a guitarist.

Le Golf Drouot was served by the metro station Richelieu Drouot… We're a duo… I thought it was perfect.

Suddenly, Richelieu Duo fell into step and started making war plans. I'd already dragged my black Telecaster out of its case and composed two or three tunes that he found convincing. "Dylan can hang it up!" All we had to do was make a demo. Since '74, we've been like a snake biting its tail, there've been so many fucking demo tapes and practice sessions. But this time I believed in it more than ever. We were up for the job! Freddy pulled out of a cupboard a '70s-era cassette deck and started to tinker with some wires.

"What, are you crazy?" I asked him.

"We're going to record on this. You'll see, the sound is excellent! Downright professional!"

This was one place I just couldn't follow him. "No, Freddy. If we make a demo, let's do it under the right conditions." While we waited for proper options, we attacked our songs, and to keep track of them, and also to make him happy, we recorded our practice sessions on his prehistoric cassette deck.

The second visit to Cherbourg was followed by a third, always on the beef heart diet.

Everyone in my life, or nearly everyone, was reasonable dubious of these Cherbourgian jaunts. Except for Atika, who encouraged me to plunge in. Most people seemed to grasp the psychological Freddy's fragility. The shrink I was seeing counseled me to keep a distance, warning me of the possibility of transference and of acting out... That didn't amuse or frighten me. In truth, I fully understood Freddy's potential dangerousness. But I've never in my life jumped out of a moving train. For me, that's something that's always struck me as dangerous.

On my third trip, Freddy had really pulled it together: he found us a recording studio. Passing by one day, he stormed in, grabbed the first guitar he saw hanging on the wall, and started to play, after which he made the owner, Donald, listen to our little demo tape of our three songs. Donald told him, "The house is yours! This house belongs to you two!" A hell of a decent guy, and also a good guitarist, Donald. A beanpole, two meters high, about our age, raised on the same mother's milk of rock of the '60s and '70s.

We set up some dates.

Back at Freddy's, it was his turn to show me his compositions. He took the occasion as an opportunity to tell me his way of seeing things, which boils down to fifty-fifty. "We'll record twelve tracks, six of yours, six of mine." That was news to me, but fine.

His songs were a gnarly mess of rapid-fire English over two chords. His voice was a raspy wood file. No use even looking for a melodic or harmonic hook. I didn't know what to say or think. In truth, I asked myself what the hell we were going to do with that. On stage, I imagined that might sound like something, but for making a demo that might show any kind of coherence to our repertoire, I had my doubts.

We headed out to the studio. Freddy and I warmed up with a little version of "Cut Across Shorty" by Eddie Cochran. And then we hit it. Donald had prepared some backing tracks based on our little home-made tape, and he added some nice guitar parts with his raw sound. He set himself up at the control panel and let us have a listen. It sounded a hell of a lot better.

We recorded my songs: *"J'ai donné," "Le renard," "Tu veux de l'or," "Âme en peine,"* and "Cheese." My voice, my guitar, Freddy's too. Then came his pieces. And there, no messing around. One take, guitar and voice. Before the chef's surprise...

Freddy had warned me on the telephone: "You won't believe it. I developed a trick... Truly original. This, nobody's done before me!" And when I saw him unpacking his gear, I really couldn't believe it. It's an electric drill! Stoic, serious, Freddy asked Donald to get him a microphone. Donald didn't say no.

"Okay, now play my tracks!" ordered Freddy, before putting on a black bandit mask, sewn with his own hands (he made another for me to wear at our concerts-to-come).

Donald reeled. And there I saw my old friend Freddy bearing down on his electric drill, marking each beat with a metronomic *vrrrrr.* Which wasn't easy—because of the trigger's inertia he had to anticipate the time by a tenth of a second.

From his mixing board, Donald sent me a look of befuddlement. Me, I thought it was funny. But it's true

that nobody's ever heard anything like that! *Vrrrr...*
Vrrrr... Vrrrr... At the end of the take, Donald
suggested that one single drill sound would do the
trick, all we'd have to do is sample it... Sample? Freddy
tossed him a condescending glance: "Bah, no!" he said.
"We need a clean blow for each measure of the song!"
Donald capitulated.

By the end of the night, and of the recording
session, we were on our knees. Freddy wouldn't let
anybody rest. He's never sleepy, he just wants to work,
work, work. Also, he never stops talking. Despite his
exhaustion and the hyper-late hour, nearly morning,
Donald, very kindly, said that we shouldn't leave empty-
handed, so he'd burn a CD of our session.

Freddy was nervous, so he took me aside. "Listen!
I don't really get what he just said. Do you mean we're
already at the stage of pressing the record?" In fact, he
was still living in the time of vinyl. The computer, the
Internet, samplers, all these modern technologies, he
maintained a contemptuous and dubious ignorance of
them. He simply didn't know what these things were
and how they worked. The proof: while we were there,
frazzled, waiting for the CD to burn, the computer
had a little bug, nothing unusual, and a little message
popped up: "fatal error." Donald didn't flinch. He'd
burn it tomorrow. He was already fried.

But Freddy jumped up and stared at the screen with
a look of terror.

"What are they saying there?"

"Who?"

"There! What's written there!"

"No, that's nothing, just a little problem with the

machine…"

"A little problem?!!! *Fatal error?!!!* You call that a little fucking problem?"

He didn't give me the time explain it to him.

"Well! Hey, that's fucking serious! Who wrote that?"

"Freddy… Nobody. That's a message that…"

"What do you mean, nobody?! Are you fucking with me, asshole? A message doesn't write itself. I want to know who the fuck is controlling that thing!"

In a flash, I saw what he saw. A Pentagon-style room, with an assembly of Kafkaesque personages seated around a table – all under the acrid eye of Big Brother. Freddy always had paranoid tendencies, which had only gotten worse with time. I was divided between pain and an urge to laugh. But Freddy wasn't joking . He went off in his madness, talking about a counter-attack, about getting our music the hell out of there, as it hadn't even been registered yet with the SACEM, out of this system of spies and vampires.

Donald began to get seriously fed up. Of Freddy, of me, and of the Richelieu Duo. Fed up of having to listen to this bullsit until five o'clock in the morning. He started to groan like a grizzly, and strangely, that seemed to have an effect.

When we got back to the garret, two deep creases of annoyance were imprinted on Freddy's brow. I was hoping to be able to collapse, finally. Another fatal error. There's my partner, pulling out all his files, all the SACEM forms he'd already filled out (four copies of each one), all the forms still to be filed, and refiled. And there he was, scribbling away like a madman, sticking sheet after sheet in front of me so I could add my signature. Some distribution agreements with percentages like 13.875 for him and the same for me, concerning our arrangements.

On the road back to Pourry, I seriously started to ask myself about the future of our duo. The disparity of our repertoires and above all the delirious side of my acolyte. Two days later, Donald sent me the CD from our recording session, and it did nothing to lift my spirits. A demo of a demo at most. But nothing you could use.

Two or three weeks go by. One morning, a call from Freddy:

"Imre! It's really serious! A bomb just exploded in my mailbox this morning!"

"Explain!"

"I just told you, a bomb exploded in my mailbox this morning!"

"Really?"

No, not really, and the more he explained, the less I understood. Or rather, I began to understand that the kid was decidedly completely off his rocker. The bomb turned out to be a letter from the SACEM, which he read to me, totally courteous and inoffensive, but he'd taken it in all the wrong ways.

"Do you understand what this means? This means that they're in the process of stealing our music!"

"But not at all, Freddy, calm down!"

"What? So you're with them too!"

"What 'them'?"

"Donald! The Internet, the SACEM, and you too, you're in it too! Now I understand! I understand that fatal error thing!!!"

Oh no… At this stage, there was nothing to discuss. I promised him that I'd call the SACEM to fix everything. And in fact I did call them. And when they heard the name of Frédérique Tchékovitch, alias Freddy Croogger, they're the ones who dropped a lead fart. Totally up to here with that fanatic harassing them with menacing phone calls and letters for the last few weeks…

A few days later, Donald called me:

"Okay, Seb! He's a really nice guy, that buddy of yours, but if he keeps fucking with me I'm going to get mad."

"What? Freddy's been fucking with you?"

"He keeps sending me death threats and telling me he's going to take legal action, and I don't have a clue what it's all about. Go ask him. Anyway, as for me, I've had about enough!"

That knocked me out. That really hurt. I felt for Donald, such a great guy, who gave us free rein of his studio and worked with us for a whole day and night. But I also felt for Freddy, totally adrift in the black stars with little chance of ever coming back again.

And suddenly, I felt for me, too. We were going nowhere. Richelieu Duo was dead.

In September there was one more exchange of phone calls, but Freddy's delirium was just increasing, his demands, his arrogance, his tone, everything became unbearable. What's more, he wouldn't call me Imre anymore – not even Seb. He reverted to Régnier, like back in high school when, for unknown reasons, he couldn't stand me.

One last phone call. I finally cracked. His tone had

become aggressive and his words were out of line. I decided to pull the plug. He was too far gone. I would have liked at least to preserve the friendship, but when I told him that, he hung up on me.

We'd come full circle. It lasted more than forty years. Nobody knows the future, but I'd put my hand in the fire to say I'm sure that Freddy and I will never see each other again.

I just hope that, for his part, he'll get the chance to see his daughter one more time...

Chapter 13
Strawberry Fields Forever

A FEW MONTHS AFTER that blissful trip to Normandy, I found myself on sabbatical, and I proposed to Imre that I go back to stay with him for a few weeks. I had an idea that we could perhaps assemble some of our adventures and some of his stories into a collaborative book. I also thought it might be a good opportunity for another musical tour. We seemed to have botched our last opportunity in France, but Europe offered some other interesting possibilities. I suggested a UK tour. I figured it was just a quick hop across the channel to get to London, a city we both love. I had a few friends there. For Imre, it held almost mythological proportions on account of his life-long obsession with British rock – The Beatles and The Stones, of course, but perhaps even more importantly, The Kinks. You can hear traces of Ray Davies through many of his songs. He also really digs early Donovan.

So, my initial thoughts were fairly straightforward: we could pop up to Paris and then take the Eurostar to London for a couple of days, hoping to score a little gig at some pub. But Imre came up with a better plan: drive up to Dieppe, on the Norman coast, and take the ferry to Brighton, where we could crash for a night or two before heading to London. I could dig it.

I wrote my UK friends and asked for possible

venues. Matthew Fink, who's a poet, wrote back suggesting a place called The George Tavern. He said something about how some other friends of his had performed there under mysterious circumstances, a story "too long to explain." Matthew's emails already tend to have an air of mystery, or at least fancy, because he signs them "Matteo" and they're always in pentameter, or at least have some other formal, usually metrical, constraint, and odd line breaks. I tend to answer in kind, just because.

The George was allegedly one of the oldest pubs in London, and for some reason struck Matteo as "suitable" for our act. When I looked the place up, there was an amazing photo of Grace Jones, which of course made me think that indeed The George Tavern was "suitable" for our act, but I wondered if they'd feel the same way about us. There was another photo on the website of Kate Moss wearing a George Tavern t-shirt. More Googling led to the legendary claim that Chaucer had been known to tie one on there in the 14th century. Dickens mentions the place in *Little Dorrit,* one of my favorite novels. I wasn't sure whom to be most excited about – Chaucer, Dickens, Grace Jones or Kate Moss – but I thought that foursome might just be our target audience. Believe it or not, when I wrote The George Tavern they agreed to put us on the bill.

Then I began scouting locations in Brighton. Hands-down the weirdest establishment seemed to be Bom-Bane's, run by a chanteuse about mid-way between Imre's age and my own. She apparently performed her original repertoire with some sort of fishbowl balanced on her head. She also readily agreed to take us in. We booked our ferry tickets and flea-bag lodgings, and got to work hammering out our set.

For the London show, we thought we'd invite a drummer to sit in – Gary, another guy of roughly our generation that we'd found through the music he posted online. Most of his archive, in fact, consisted not of his own playing, but rather of old recordings of his brother, Brian, who had passed away fairly recently – under what circumstances we didn't know. What we did know was that Brian, like Imre, was the kind of artist that made you scratch your head and wonder why the hell you'd never heard of him before. Nearly all of his songs had the ring of classics. I'd done covers of a couple of them, and Imre had made a French version of another. We were in agreement that the guy was an astonishment. Gary, for his part, was pretty self-effacing, only modestly admitting his musicianship on some tracks – though he sounded very capable – and personally, like a prince of a guy. When we invited him to join us for the gig, he accepted.

We set out on a blustery, late-summer morning to Dieppe. The Normandy coast can get pretty warm at that time of year, but that week had been more like a typical April – cool winds and scattered showers. Imre warned me that Brighton was likely to be chillier still. The channel crossing started out smoothly enough – that is, the water was a bit choppy, but nothing to write home about. We stood on the upper deck as we sailed out of Dieppe. Imre was staring back at the cliffs of Varengeville, and he had that Viking look he sometimes gets. Inside, it was pretty comfortable. There were padded chairs and little coffee tables scattered around, and they were populated by a mix of young families and older couples. It struck us that many people were involved in activities that required no electronic apparatus at all – reading paperbacks, writing in notebooks, knitting, and doing crossword puzzles. I'd brought some knitting myself. Imre always has a notebook. We reasoned that anybody who'd cross the channel on a boat a) had some time on his or her hands and b) had a certain taste for doing things the old-fashioned way. The ferry seems a bit antiquated – but from what we could see, it was perfectly civilized, and reasonably efficient: three hours' crossing from Dieppe to Brighton.

Well, that was the scheduled travel time anyway. But shortly after we'd settled into our comfy seats, a woman announced over a loudspeaker, first in French, then in English, that any trained medical workers were urgently needed for a passenger in distress. We noticed a couple of people jumping up to help. A low-grade anxiety settled over us all, and held for an hour or so, until another announcement came on saying that due to this passenger's dire condition, she would need to be evacuated by helicopter, so we were going to have to hold still for a little while until that could happen. This would affect our arrival time, but they couldn't yet tell us by how much. Actually, they didn't identify the passenger as female, but we happened to be sitting near one of the British nurses who had offered her services, and we overheard her explaining that a woman appeared to be having a heart attack. She seemed to think she'd be okay, but evidently it was better for her to be flown back to France than to wait to be hospitalized in Britain.

The ferry stopped moving. We could feel the

engines running, but we were just sitting still there, apparently right smack in the middle of the channel. It was a very strange sensation. It felt as if time itself were suspended. We never actually heard the helicopter landing on the top deck.

So I can't really tell you how long we were sitting there in a daze like that, but when they finally updated us on the implications for our arrival time, they said we'd be about three hours late. Yikes. We'd given ourselves not much wiggle-room in advance of our gig in Brighton. Now it appeared we'd be getting to shore just minutes before showtime. We'd still need to get a bus from the port of Newhaven to the town proper, and then drop our things off at the hotel. Both Imre and I had a very tenuous cellular connection on the boat, so we each sent a message to Jane, the proprietress of Bom-Bane's, explaining our plight.

We didn't actually think she'd be too upset. When we'd written her the day before saying we were looking forward to meeting her, she wrote back warning us that "nobody had booked" anything for the evening so she wasn't sure there would be any audience at all. She said it nicely. Our feelings weren't particularly hurt. We hadn't exactly papered the town with publicity, and who the hell knew who we were in Brighton anyway?

But once we'd docked, things moved pretty quickly. We hopped on a bus and checked in to our hotel. We texted Jane to say that we'd pop over as soon as we could, just to say hello, and if it made any sense, maybe we could still play a tune or two, and if not, no problem. But as we were unloading our stuff in our room, Imre started to waffle even on that plan. He said

202

the prolonged boat ride had left him a little wobbly. He thought maybe we could just drop it. I did something I rarely do: I mildly guilt-tripped him.

Good call. Bom-Bane's was a magical little terrarium of a place, and Jane was altogether as quirky as she'd appeared on the Internet.

Her place was tiny, but full up with cheery patrons drinking and dining. There were peculiar paintings on the walls, and the aforementioned fishbowl-like assemblages that revealed themselves, on further inspection, to be elaborate headgear. Jane later explained to us that she liked to make fanciful hats, and often used them as thematic illustrations for her compositions.

She offered us a drink, and invited us to take a seat in the corner and play. She said, "Here's the musical act that was delayed!" We jumped into our set. Despite his initial resistance, Imre was cheered by the warm applause, and pretty soon we were on a roll. At one point, a table of three middle-aged hens (as they call ladies in the UK) started to giggle. I thought perhaps it was Imre's slightly dirty lyrics, but between songs they pointed out that the table at which we were seated seemed to be "having a reaction" to our playing – moving slowly but perceptibly up and down. This was evidently a little motor-controlled trick of Jane's. There was another table with a clockwork-like operation under the glass moving around small plastic replicas of the amusement park rides on the Brighton boardwalk.

After our set, we chit-chatted with the patrons and checked out a lengthy framed "sad but true" poem of Jane's on the wall, which had been illustrated with those peculiar paintings. It was the troubling story of a young girl who had, with her sister, made a stuffed toy man named "Guy". Unfortunately, her mother found him somehow objectionable, and threw him into the fire. Guy was incinerated. Jane said that the little girl grew up to have serial difficulties in love, often precipitating the end of relationships prematurely. She said that psychotherapists had had various hypotheses of the reason for her problems with intimacy, but that she knew that it all stemmed from the incineration of her beloved Guy.

Later we looked at some old pictures of Jane online, and listened to some of her old songs. One was called, "I've Lost My Sheen." She appeared to have been very beautiful as a young woman – in fact, she still was. We found her songs enchanting. She said she liked ours, too.

The next day we explored the town. Imre had spent a few days in Brighton years ago on a holiday with his younger son Martin, and he had fond memories. It really is delightful. We ambled around the pier, which is a bit like Coney Island, and took a ride on the ferris wheel.

We also visited the Royal Pavilion, which was once a vacation resort of the royals. The architecture is in the Indian style, which is weird if you think about it. There were lots of Britons taking pictures of themselves in front of the Pavilion. Actually, I took a picture of Imre, too. But watching that spectacle of self-documentation before the remnants of England's colonial past, Imre knit his brow and said, *"la nostalgie…"*

It was perhaps a little judgmental, as an observation regarding the Britons' attitude toward the period of Empire, but Imre was the first to admit to his own nostalgic tendencies in the UK, which really came to the fore when we got to London. This had to do with his own regular pilgrimages there in his youth. It had been nearly twenty years since his last visit, but in his teens and early twenties he went there all the time to see shows and buy records. The thing is, his obsession with British rock of the '60s and '70s is by no means singular. That's the music that seemed to be playing everywhere we went. We walked past a little gaggle of drunk young men outside a pub and they were singing "A Hard Day's

Night."

Oh, I forgot to mention that the little inn we stayed at in Brighton was called Strawberry Fields.

I should say a bit more about our preparation for the London gig. My friends in London had been, as I said, very helpful with the suggestion of a venue, but sadly, they'd be out of town on the day of our gig. Matthew wrote us in advance, while we were still in Normandy, to apologize. He and his partner, PA, had decamped to Cupi, Tuscany, "where," he reported in hexameter, "the furnace-like / heat has annihilated the ambition to move." He advised us to fill The George with as many of our "partisans" as possible, since "The greatest drawback of performing in a pub / is that the customers tend to be really blotto."

I wrote back in my habitual if paltry five metrical feet: "I'm sorry too you won't be at the gig / but we will raise a glass to you and P / A. Our friends are all impressed as hell / that we'll be playing at a bar where Chaucer / purportedly got sauced. Our warm regards! / We ate a jellied pig's foot in the garden!" That was true. Imre had just been introducing me to some local Norman specialties that day. Believe it or not, the *pied de cochon en gelée* was the easiest to get down. There was also *museau*, which is snout – and a liqueur called *Get 27* which looked and tasted like Scope. Seriously, that was the worst.

Anyway, now that we were facing the gig, it appeared that our "partisans" would consist of Gary's family. Another brother, Terry, and his wife Jo were giving us a ride over, and a sister, Jayne, and some nieces met us at the club. They were really lovely, and very warm.

That may give you the impression of a lot of family solidarity, and indeed, they seem to be extremely close-knit. Part of this solidarity expresses itself around the loss of Brian. Before we went on, Gary gestured to his wristwatch and said, "This was Bri's watch, I always wear it when I play," and they all nodded wistfully. Terry said, "That's how he keeps time." Jayne said, "And the glasses!" Gary pulled out a pair of John Lennon-style shades that had also belonged to Brian.

But I think they were also coming out that night for Gary. It was something of a big deal for him to be playing out – it had been about fifteen years. He said he had some social anxieties. Imre empathized. I asked Gary if he knew Imre's song, "I Hate Parties." He said, "I love that one."

As I mentioned, Gary's close in age to Imre, and he shares much of his musical taste as well. He also loves The Kinks, and he told us he met them once, back in the day. He said, "It's too bad they couldn't get along, Ray and Dave." The Davies brothers. It's true, everybody says that – they used to famously fight on stage, and in interviews they were constantly either bashing or bemoaning each other. Unlike, obviously, Gary, whose fraternal devotion appeared to be a central anchor of his existence. Imre said he'd seen a documentary clip in which Ray Davies said that when he was sick in the hospital for months, all he could think about was how much he wanted his brother to visit him. Finally, he did.

Still, when I checked online about the Davies brothers' "feud," there were some pretty choice recent quotations from Dave about his brother Ray: "You've heard of vampires. Well, Ray sucks me dry of ideas, emotions and creativity. It's toxic for me to be with him. He's a control freak." "We must be careful. We might be feeding Ray's illness by making him think he's more interesting than he is." When asked to identify Ray's illness: "He's a narcissist." "I think Ray has been happy for only three years in his life. And those were the three years before I was born."

But someplace else he said, "I love my brother."

Well. How did our gig go? It was sweet. There were a couple of other acts – a Malagasy French girl who'd also brought out her whole family – she sang country songs in English – a young British woman of Caribbean descent with a striking voice and a hammer technique on guitar, a very young British rocker guy who laughed somewhat hysterically between his mournful howling songs – and us, the oddball elders.

I introduced us, making reference to our own diverse points of origin, and we crooned, plucked and shuffled our way through our set. The crowd, which, let's face it, was basically constituted by two large and supportive families, didn't seem particularly "blotto." We stuck around for a bit until Imre's own mild social phobia set in, and we hugged everybody and headed back to our hotel.

The next day we went to see the Turner collection at the Tate. Imre and I both love Turner. If you stand back from the paintings, you get entirely lost in the landscapes, you feel sucked into them, but if you look more closely, you see they're actually very weird and apparently haphazard blobs of oil – they don't look painted at all, but like somebody made a mess. How did he do that? Imre, as I've said, has a mystical relationship to nature, so that "getting lost" experience is quite profound for him. When we felt really saturated with Turner, we went into the Blake gallery. They were contemporaries, of course, and both visionaries, but so radically different in their originality, it's hard to believe they were living in the same time and place. The wall text said that Blake's highly innovative engravings were "inspired" by his recently deceased brother. I stared and stared at those, and thought about Gary, and Brian, and Ray and Dave Davies.

The next day we went back to Brighton to catch our ferry back to Normandy. The station was very chaotic, and they told us to get on without standing in line to pick up our tickets as they were just rushing people through on account of the crowds. We were confused until we got off at Brighton and realized that we'd landed smack dab in the middle of their enormous annual Gay Pride Celebration. Brighton had already struck us as pretty admirably queer, and now it was jam-packed with rainbow-bedecked revelers. We wriggled our way through the crowds down to the stony beach, which was strewn with colorful lesbians and pink-haired boys in suspenders. The sun was finally shining, brilliantly.

We sat on the stones, and combed our hands through them. I found some beautiful white shells, polished down into the shapes of tiny ears. They reminded me of a friend's baby, the one I'd been knitting booties for on the boat. The baby's name is Leonora, and she has small, lovely ears that look just like those shells.

It was time to go, so we walked back to Churchill Square to catch our bus to the ferry. The bus system was also in a state of mayhem, but somehow we managed to sardine ourselves into one and make it back to the Newhaven port in the nick of time. For all the melancholy thinking about the past on this trip, somehow those colorful young people in Brighton and those tiny ear-shaped shells had pointed us to something that felt, sweetly, like the future. This time the waters were utterly peaceful. We stood on the deck at the stern and watched the sun setting behind us. There was something profoundly right, this time, about looking back, but also feeling ourselves moving forward.

Lodbrog's Epilogue

WHEN, AFTER HAVING TOLD HER his story, I showed Bébé those images of Freddy that I'd shot in Cherbourg, that madman in his bandit mask with the electric drill in the studio, that beautiful savage with his silvery hair tearing up the fretboard of his "Daphne," she cried. Right there in New York, she'd suddenly taken in, better than she could have through my storytelling, the actual dimensions of that pathetic loser set adrift by his talent and lost in the world. But, without going into details, I don't think Freddy would have loved New York – at least not the West Village. And I don't think New York would have loved Freddy.

It's sometimes with his eyes that I myself look at this little socio-cultural bubble, version 2015. Apart from the Bowery and its vestiges of the Court of Miracles (which he would have fled like the plague after his years in the streets), Freddy would have been revolted by the ostentatious luxury that announces itself everywhere. The arty good life of Soho and its surroundings would have made his blood boil. As for the universe of performance art, that really would have put him over the edge…

Me, I love New York as much as ever. Since March of 2014, I've spent about half my time here and I feel more and more a part of it. I have a membership card for the public pool around the corner. I have "my bench" in Washington Square Park where I go to daydream, I have my little haunts where I like to walk, and pick up a few things for my daughters, and I even have a French bakery down the block where I go once in a while to buy us some croissants.

Bébé's friends have become my friends, and I'm touched by the warm way in which they've integrated me into their circle. All beautiful people. As I was getting to know them, I noted with some surprise that in each apartment in which I found myself, the bookshelves were invariably lined with Derrida, Deleuze, Barthes, Foucault and company – something you don't often see in France. What's more, New Yorkers in general seem to me so kind, so courteous, in contrast to our badgering Parisians, too often injected with aggressivity. Here, one smiles at you in the street, one makes small talk in the elevator, if someone bumps into you in the street they apologize, and the person at the check-out in the supermarket asks you how you're doing.

Still, as an African proverb goes, "Leave a tree trunk in the water for a thousand years and it still won't become a crocodile." I'll never be a New Yorker. Too Parisian in my bowels and my brain. I love differences. If one knows how to take them, they can bring people together rather than pushing them apart. So perhaps now is the right time to point out a few differences I've experienced in New York.

On the cultural plane, there's much more than the six hours dividing America from France. There are centuries as deep as the Atlantic Ocean. Between me and Bébé, that's occasionally provoked … There's a word in the American language that I've discovered, and

I love its sound, but not its meaning. Glitch. Literally, a little system error. There's another word, but of this one I'd say I love neither the sound *nor* the meaning: spat. As far as I can tell, it seems to come from the past tense of the word "to spit." In short, these two words mean about the same thing – a light skid, giving way to a little conflict. We've had a few of these little glitches, Bébé and I.

But I've always been attracted by what's new. And I've certainly been served my share here. For me, being parachuted into the West Village has been a trip worthy of Voltaire's *Candide*. We are in the sphere of performance art. Bébé is a professor of Performance Studies at NYU, and I'm fucking speechless every time I try to explain to my friends what that means. It's that the term "performance" here seems to have nothing to do with its definition in French. So, I've gone to see any number of performances with Bébé, in the form of diverse spectacles that left me with highly contrasted impressions, sometimes enthusiastic, sometimes perplexed – once in a while mildly outraged. I was occasionally dumbstruck by the fact that what intellectuals here celebrate would incite the throwing of tomatoes on the other side of the Atlantic.

That's when an abyss seems to open between Bébé and me, she the modern American, me (as Dick Cheney liked to put it) the old European, each one with his or her baggage, history, and education. As for what I've discovered aesthetically in this world of performance art, I really would like to love everything. But that isn't the case, and I can't hide my feelings. If, on rare occasions, that's created some friction between Bébé and me, I've

213

quickly come to understand that, very often, she takes things to heart. Most of the time, the performers are her friends or her students. So we're appreciating things on different levels.

Once, we went to a concert by two of her students. A great little female punk rock duo, bass and drums, with singing. The name of the group? Penis. In France, with a name like that, one would feel obliged to add a nasty, provocative edge to the form. Not in New York. The provocation is intellectual, and it branches out into smiles. That speaks without words. I loved Penis.

What I love a little less are some of the intentionally disconcerting demonstrations that, under the pretext of conceptualism, claim the status of art. An endless crawl along the floor intended to evoke one's own birth, for instance. And once, under theatrical lighting, a trio seated on three chairs. A young woman, microphone in hand, set herself to interviewing the two guys on either side of her, passing them the microphone. The older of the two, sporting a goatee and horn-rimmed glasses, was a psychoanalyst. The second was a magician. Questioned by this woman who I figured was some sort of journalist, each of them responded expansively, saying, as far as I could tell, very little that was of much interest. I figured that this was some sort of promotional or introductory interview and I waited to see what would happen next. Then I learned, on leaving, that that *was* the performance – in fact, a "choreography." Dance. Well! So that was art.

Where does art begin and where does it end? I cited that slogan of May '68 – "Art is shit." In the spirit of the epoch, that meant a bourgeois concept directly inherited from the time of privilege, and that had to be destroyed by henchmen. That's stupid. Guernica! Art is above all, for me, a kind of oxygen without which it would be impossible to even survive in the fucking system. An essential nutrient. That's why I'm so distrustful of counterfeits... My suspicion has sometimes turned to exasperation, when I had the sense that I was being taken for a fool, held emotional hostage in an intellectual scam, divested of my most basic sense of modesty. Even if I had no doubt of the sincerity of the artists in question.

Downtown, thematically, erotic eclecticism occupies, generally, a place of honor. On stage, and apparently in the street, heterosexuality is the exception. Nothing wrong with that. Still, I can't help think *in petto* of the poor gays working in some factory in the sticks, or living in certain cities in the southern hemisphere. It's good to inhale this perfume of extroverted liberty, this spirited openness and this tolerance so cruelly lacking in our "old Europe."

Perhaps the various blockages I've experienced could be boiled down to one thing: my resistance to the overexposure of *Me*, and thus of the *Ego,* through the *I*. I quickly came to realize that all of that arose from the principle, in fact the conviction, that the *I*, beyond being a narcissistic end-point, was supposed to be an object of fascination for the other. I have nothing against the *I*, which, in literature, often becomes an entirely different character – not to speak of memoires and autobiographies, in which it creates a powerful form of identification with the reader. But when it becomes a cultural alibi, a kind of avant-garde rule of thumb, that's when I lose it. I remember the counsel given by Oscar Wilde to André Gide one day as they were out walking together: "The *I* should be banished from all forms of art!" Unless that famous *I* might become *You*.

For other reasons, but not unrelated ones, I get a little bugged by the way New Yorkers think about poetry and poets. In the '60s, the Beat Generation was all about poetry. In the '80s, the punks, Patti Smith at the head of the crowd, reclaimed Rimbaud and Verlaine. They went straight to the source.

Today? As with art, I ask myself: What is poetry? And the answer that comes to me is: Something unconscious of itself. What is a poet? Someone who doesn't know he or she is one. So how can one put this bird in a cage and call oneself a poet? I confess that I was a bit shocked to hear this appellation become, in New York, a self-assigned title, a social status, even a profession – which is precisely the opposite of the lunar or saturnine Pierrot, with his nose always in the air, his feet never on the ground, which is, for me, the poet. I think again of Marie-Isabelle, whose sweetness would turn to fury at the idea of calling herself a poetess. And yet she left behind such beautiful poems. Well! Each of us writes some poems in our lives, but not everybody is a poet. And that's all for the best, in a sense – otherwise society would crumble and the world would stop spinning.

But enough of these little notes of discord! Enough glitches! One would have to be a real pig to spit in this soup! What I see in New York, my days and nights there, Bleecker Street with its ghosts, the sun hitting those glass towers, the fishmonger's stall on Canal Street, that baby in a kangaroo carrier whose father took him to see a Matisse exhibit, that magnificent street character, a Viet Nam vet, with the profile of a prophet... All of that is truly poetry.

And between Bébé and me, I'm not worried. Despite our differences, there are a few sure values that hold us together, and the bridges continue to multiply. She loves Montaigne, I love Penis, we both love oysters and beer. And when I showed her those images of Freddy, Bébé cried.

I think that one's life is the most faithful mirror in which to regard oneself, and recognize oneself, or not. I've never understood if life was short and passing slowly, or if it was long and passing quickly. One thing is sure, it's passing. Pathologically tortured by time since my early childhood, I've tried to capture it in slices, like with those millions of photos I've taken that I'll never look at again, or in the intimate journal I've kept nearly every day since 5 August 1969. It's added up to a mountain of Clairefontaine notebooks (I'm faithful to the brand) – more than eleven thousand pages. Why such an enterprise? It's as though I feared a brutal amnesia which might abolish my memory from one moment to the next. An instantaneous case of Alzheimer's. All those recollections consigned to black and white would be a manner of holding on to them, should such a thing ever happen. But what could be stupider? Because what use would reminiscences be if they were cut off from memory? Why, then, blacken all those pages that I'd never have time to reread? It would take another lifetime, and I would have other things to do.

On the other hand, I can plunge into nearly fifty years of notes and decipher old relations, friendships, loves. I can go back to the source. I can trace a chain of haphazard events and connections that results in this "here and now." A few events with apparently no great importance, like, for example, 7 January 2014: "Before taking the train, I wrote a little song for a stranger, and I posted it on SoundCloud. Barbara Browning is the name of the stranger, and the title of the song."

Since she asked me in that early email, "Who made you up?," it's been nearly two years, that bottle of Vouvray's been emptied, and a few others as well. Did I answer the question? It would have been difficult to do away with the *I* in this story, which was written largely in the first person singular. But it's not by chance that I chose to tell my story through Freddy's.

His is the story I wanted to tell, because that amazing musician, that creased and weathered man, immune to all sorts of facile seductions, pursuing an inaccessible star, is an emblematic figure for me. In my eyes, he represents the Revolutionary par excellence. The one who preaches no dogma, but refuses to compromise. Guys like him, and there aren't many of them, truly put into focus our rotten system, even if they have to sacrifice themselves in the process. "Why don't losers ever win?" asked JJ Cale. Maybe because the losers don't want to win. They were programed otherwise. I might even go so far as to say that Freddy's failure was his success. And also, without Freddy, there couldn't have been Lodbrog, and that would have been a damned shame for Sébastien Régnier. My meeting with Bébé streamed directly and strangely from my trips to Cherbourg.

Our story is as beautiful as it was impossible to

imagine. In 1933, a little girl is born in Tokyo. Seven years later, in Liverpool, it's the moment for a little badass, son of a sailor, to come into the world. John Lennon and Yoko Ono. My mother was Transylvanian, my father Norman. It's not by chance that he adored that song by Lennon, "You are Here." It evokes love born under the sign of chance. "From Liverpool to Tokyo, what a way to go... From distant lands, one woman, one man, let the four winds blow..." Encounters that had no chance of occurring, but that occurred, across distance and time. Which gives them a particular aura, a strange sense of destiny. Me, the newborn Paris baby in the 1950s, Bébé, at the dawn of the 60s, being born in Wisconsin...

One day, maybe I'll write a book with the title *Who the Hell is Barbara Browning?* It would be a worthy subject. Bébé doesn't like it when I speak too adoringly of her. So I'm going to take advantage of the situation while her back is turned and quickly throw it all down here. Bébé is beautiful, Bébé is funny, very funny, sensitive, sensual, fragile, and solid. Her spirit sparkles as if it's been polished like a gemstone. Bébé calls herself a communist. At first that made me jump, but in fact she takes the term back to its proper definition, that of sharing, and of equity. That translates into a generosity without boundaries, and it clearly doesn't limit itself to the material plane. I've seen her and I see her with her students – she gathers them, invites them, advises and accompanies them like a mother hen with her chicks.

With me, considering the disparity of our circumstances, this generosity at first put me ill at ease, but ended up piercing my armor of false dignity. She taught me to accept. Bébé has a good heart – too good sometimes, and under certain circumstances. She can lose sight of her own interests while looking out for the other, and sometimes she finds herself in difficult situations when she doesn't know how to set boundaries. Bébé is a committed and engaged feminist. Having encountered certain aggressive and vindictive offshoots of the French *Mouvement de Libérations des Femmes*, where the simple fact of being a man had sometimes made me feel something like the accused facing a tribunal, I discovered through her a feminism with a human face – in fact, based on the same principles as her communism: sharing, and equity.

Our story has shifted both our courses. It's true that at the outset, I had some reservations regarding sexuality. Nothing against the thing itself, of course, but the concept. I'd always lived it as something secret, something instinctive and animal, impossible to speak of and in any event inseparable from my old romantic ideals. After one of our first feverish nights, Bébé said to me – and meant it to make me happy – "I love our sex!" To which I responded, almost grumpily, "Me, I call that making love!"

For her part, Bébé wasn't always completely comfortable on the sentimental plane. Maybe, as she explains it, because of a kind of inverted modesty. Or maybe it felt like a threat to her liberty. Without going into details, I think I can say that each one of us has made a pretty big move in the direction of the other.

And it was Bébé who came up with this strange idea to make Imre Lodbrog actually exist in the world. Maybe there was something quixotic about the task, but she set herself to it heart and soul, and with all of her imagination, digging with a shovel through the rocky garden of my life of artistic activities and ambitions. After her crazy initiative to make me come to New York for the first time to sing at the Hôtel Particulier, passing through that Eastern European Tour that she pulled out of her hat, and on to other projects to come, she's been constantly on the prowl for the next gig, stringing together possibilities in every direction… Why? I think it's just because she loves my songs. For my part, I haven't forgotten that I left off reading her novels mid-course. If it was too early in February of 2014, maybe now's the time. As much as I wanted to cling to mystery back then, I'm just as avid now to understand her.

"Will you still need me, will you still feed me, when I'm sixty-four?" My sixty-fourth birthday is in six months. And that's the question I'm tempted to sing to Bébé. But, as if anticipating the question, sensing my occasional anxiety that all this might just be a dream, soon to evaporate, she set her sights much further, and composed for me that pretty little lullaby: "We Have Twenty-Nine Years."

So, I let myself be lulled. Whatever the terrible blows that life can inflict on us, I've never had more appetite for it. The same goes for Lodbrog.

Salut à toi, Freddy! Wherever you are.

About the authors

Barbara Browning is the author of *The Gift (or Techniques of the Body)*, *The Correspondence Artist* and *I'm Trying to Reach You*. Sébastien Régnier is a French song and screenwriter and winner of the French Grand Prize for Best Screenplay for *Kabloonak*.

CPSIA information can be obtained
at www.ICGtesting.com
Printed in the USA
BVOW11s2245100118
504883BV00003B/6/P